Common Heritage of Mankind:

A Bibliography of Legal Writing

by

Prue Taylor and Lucy Stroud

PUBLISHED BY FONDATION DE MALTE

Casa Cintraj, 54 West Street, Valletta, VLT 1536, Malta

ISBN: 978-1-291-57725-9

Email address: info@fondationdemalte.org
Website: www.fondationdemalte.org

in collaboration with

the European Centre for Information on Marine Science and Technology

Father Peter Serracino Inglott

(1936 - 2012)

Table of Contents

FOREWORD

This bibliography of legal writing on the Common Heritage of Mankind (CHM) is dedicated to the memory of Father Peter Serracino Inglott (1936-2012). Father Peter worked together with Elisabeth Mann Borgese and Arvid Pardo to elucidate the content of the Common Heritage and advocate for its use. Father Peter's deep understanding of Christian theology and the philosophy of Thomas Aquinas enabled him to make a unique contribution. He understood the need to explore and explain the moral foundations of the Common Heritage and its links with natural law theory. Encapsulating an ancient wisdom about the responsibilities of humanity, he considered that it could and should evolve to address new global challenges.

Having worked for more than half a century side by side with Father Peter, I shared his dedication to the Common Heritage of Mankind.

For Father Peter, the doctrine of the Common Heritage of Mankind was the cornerstone of the UNESCO project on human responsibilities. He inspired me to launch this project in 1980 when I was the UNESCO director for socio-environmental affairs. The project concerned the rights of future generations to their environment and we drafted a declaration thereon that was eventually approved by UNESCO's General Conference in 1997 (Declaration on the Responsibilities of the Present Generations Towards Future Generations).[1]

Father Peter had already advised the then Prime Minister of Malta, Dr George Borg Olivier, that Malta should suggest to the United Nations, through the powerful voice of Arvid Pardo (then Malta's Permanent Delegate to the UN) and with the influential support of Elisabeth Mann Borgese, that seabed resources lying beyond national jurisdiction should be declared as forming part of the common patrimony of humankind to be developed for peaceful purposes in an environmentally sustainable manner. This led to Pardo's historic 1967 speech to the United Nations outlining an ocean management strategy that declared the deep seabed, ocean floor and its resources as the Common Heritage of Mankind.[2]

At a party at my house, some months later, Father Peter cornered the Prime Minister and Arvid advocating that Malta should forthwith announce

---

[1] Resolution 44 adopted on 12 November 1997 by the General Conference of UNESCO at its 29th Session (Paris).
[2] United Nations, General Assembly Official Records, First Committee, 22nd Session (New York), UN Docs. A/C.I/PV. 1515 and A/C.I/PV. 1516 (1 November, 1967). See also UN Doc. A/6695 (18 August 1967).

its intention to move that the Declaration of Principles Governing the Sea-Bed and the Ocean Floor[3] be adopted by the United Nations, despite skeptical attitudes already shown by some Member States. The United States ambassador had wondered who was behind Malta's 'mischievous' initiative!

Father Peter considered that a new social and economic world order had necessarily to espouse such a declaration and to render it meaningful through the appropriate institutional arrangements, particularly the creation of an authority to supervise and monitor seabed matters. He had wanted to extend the concept to all ocean issues as well as to promote the attendant principle that the technology required to exploit ocean resources should be equally accepted as forming part of the CHM - a notion eagerly advanced by Elisabeth Mann Borgese and myself largely through the proposal, eventually made by the Government of Malta to the UN, for the creation of Meditech - a pan-Mediterranean cooperative project to foster technological research related to marine resources.[4]

---

[3] Declaration of Principles Governing the Sea-Bed and the Ocean Floor, and the Subsoil Thereof, Beyond the Limits of National Jurisdiction. United Nations General Assembly Resolution 2749 (XXV) of 17 December 1970, GAOR, 25th Session (New York), Supp. No. 28, UN Doc. A/8028.

[4] Salvino Busuttil and Pierangelo Catalano (eds) *Euro-Mediterranean Technological Cooperation: With Special Reference to Marine*

In all these parallel issues, Father Peter was an enthusiastic fellow-traveller and often ahead of Elisabeth (whom he identified, a few months before he passed away, as the most defining person in his life).

For him, Common Heritage was a basic tenet of his own Christian faith, but one which applied to all men and women irrespective of their creeds and convictions. As a believer, for Peter (who always clarified that he was first and foremost a Priest) that patrimony came directly from the Father who exercised *patria potestas* on all creation, endowing humankind with the rights and responsibilities of stewardship through a *ius utendi*.

In that transcendent vision, we celebrate his life and, with hope, we dream of the realization of his cherished de Chardin vista of all creation, merging in the fullness of time with its Creator in whose image we are all moulded, embracing a heritage by Him legated.

Salvino Busuttil
President, Fondation de Malte

Technology (Foundation for International Studies, University of Malta, Valletta, 1993) Annexes 1-3.

INTRODUCTION

In 1967, the Maltese lawyer Arvid Pardo launched the concept of the Common Heritage of Mankind (CHM) onto the international stage. His November speech to the United Nations General Assembly has become a common starting point for legal discussion on the CHM and the substance of legend. His task was to introduce the international community to an ethical concept and to formulate the legal principles needed to implement it. The particular context was growing concern for the future of the world's oceans and associated concern for peace, ecological health and growing social and economic inequality. He was later to describe his role in the following terms:

"Lawyers, who are attentive to the presence of great material wealth located in distant areas now open to exploration, use, and exploitation are obliged to formulate new legal principles, or to modify old ones, in order that these newly found and available natural resources may be used to the benefit of all mankind. The nature of the world's political structure ... has materially changed in recent years. Under such circumstances an appropriate function of lawyers is to comprehend the reality which surrounds them. Equipped with such an understanding they are entitled to propose legal principles designed to meet to the maximum extent possible – taking into account all of the challenges of the ecological age – the needs, wants, interests and values of individuals and of society at large. ...[CHM] takes into account the precepts of distributive justice. It, by definition, is a creative approach and contains within itself those qualities enabling it to become a guardian of valid interests."[1]

The passage and evolution of CHM, through the UN Committee on the Peaceful Uses of the Seabed and the Ocean Floor Beyond the Limits of National Jurisdiction, the UN Conference on the Law of the Sea (UNCLOS III) negotiations and the 1994 Implementation Agreement (to Part XI of UNCLOS) is well known and the subject of comprehensive (often conflicting) commentary and analysis. Equally, its presence in the 1967 Outer Space Treaty and the 1979 Moon Treaty is also well documented. Contemporary discussion on international environmental law frequently refers to its rejection in the context of the 1992 Rio conventions on climate change and biodiversity. In the place of CHM, the phrases 'common concern' and 'common interest' have emerged. But have

---

[1] Arvid Pardo and Carl Q Christol "The Common Interest: Tension Between the Whole and the Parts" in Ronald StJ Macdonald and Douglas M Johnston (eds) *The Structure and Process of International Law: Essays in Legal Philosophy, Doctrine and Theory* (Martinus Nijhoff Publishers, The Hague, 1983) 643 at 658.

they served or undermined the task of articulating our collective responsibility for the common good? Users of this bibliography will find a rich array of perspectives and a wealth of new knowledge and detail covering the many aspects of CHM.

While much is known and has been written about the CHM, what is less well known is that Arvid Pardo belonged to a team of thinkers, all of whom informed CHM's development and shaped a strategy for its acceptance into international law. Father Peter Serracino Inglott (to whom this work is dedicated), together with Elisabeth Mann Borgese (the First Lady of the Oceans), worked alongside Arvid Pardo. In later years, Salvino Busuttil played a pivotal role in the context of UNESCO and in furthering the understanding of and scholarship on inter-generational equity. Each of these individuals brought their own unique talents to the task of championing CHM, but it is the fruit of a truly collective endeavor. One key component of the strategy for CHM was that the starting point, for its introduction into international law, would be the resources of the oceans beyond national jurisdiction. This was a pragmatic decision attributed to the politics of the time. But from there, it was the hope and intention that, like the concentric circles created by a stone (or water droplet) dropped into still water, its scope and influence would ripple around the Earth. Elisabeth Mann Borgese described the task in these words:

"If the oceans are indeed man's last frontier on this old earth of scarcity and competition to which we have reduced our common heritage, the law of the seas is the advance post on the long march toward a new world of science and technology, of abundance and cooperation, which we have set out to achieve."[2]

All these people have stayed true to this vision, not in a naïve sense but with the true strength of conviction that comes from knowing that the CHM embraces a moral force that unifies humanity and is *capable* of generating an integrated or coherent "view of ourselves in our environment that is both new and old and that departs from uniquely Europocentric, Western tradition and attempts to blend Western scientific values with Eastern philosophical values".[3] That this vision for the future has not yet come to fruition was not so much a disappointment but rather (as Elisabeth described it) an indication that the 'philosophical setting' for CHM is not yet in place.[4] Neither Elisabeth nor Father Peter were deterred by this, rather both shared a positive view of human beings

---

[2] Elisabeth Mann Borgese and David Krieger (eds) *The Tides of Change: Peace, Pollution, and Potential of the Oceans* (Mason/Charter, New York, 1975) 352.

[3] Elisabeth Mann Borgese *The Future of the Oceans: A Report to the Club of Rome* (Harvest House, Montréal, 1986) 131.

[4] Ibid, 125-134.

– as capable and destined to understand that the individual resides in community with all others, including the greater community of all life. In this conviction they shared much with Thomas Berry who spoke so eloquently of our ability to recognize ourselves as members of a larger community of life and to develop a primary allegiance to the flourishing of that community.[5]

This bibliography of academic writing on CHM takes 1967 as its starting point. What it demonstrates, by its scope, volume and by the nationalities of the authors, is that contrary to the opinion of those who dismiss CHM as 'dead and buried on the deep seabed' (at best) or merely a political slogan or utopian ideal (at worst), CHM is indeed alive and flourishing. It is continuing to inform and guide thinking and debate across an increasing array of topics ranging from marine living resources to the humane genome, from Antarctica to natural and cultural heritage. This is consistent with the foresight of Arvid Pardo (and others), who considered CHM flexible enough to adapt to the emerging challenges, the discovery of new resources and values, such as scientific research.[6]

---

[5] Thomas Berry *The Dream of the Earth* (Sierra Club Books, California, 1988) 42-43.
[6] Antony J Dolman *Resources, Regimes, World Order* (Pergamon Press, New York, 1981) 227-228.

One of the key aspects of CHM, that underpins the range of topics to which it is being applied and links it with an important debate in international law, is that of 'human responsibility' for the collective good. In this respect, CHM is highly relevant to the task of developing a 'responsibility based approach' to law. It might be explained in these terms: we, current generations of humanity, have the individual and collective responsibility to preserve the fundaments of life for the benefit of all. This embraces the notion of concern and respect for the 'other'. This is most often expressed in the context of human relationships (intra- and inter-generational equity), but can also be understood to encompass the relationship between humans and nature. This eco-centric understanding of CHM was, in the view of Father Peter, most evident in the context of the human genome project. It has given us scientific proof of what we have long known, but through hubris have periodically denied, that there is unity to all life on Earth.

An example of the potential of CHM, to restore the balance between a 'responsibility based approach' to law with the dominant 'rights based approach', is contained in the 1997 UNESCO Declaration on the Responsibilities of the Present

Generations Towards Future Generations[7] and in the Maltese initiative of a draft Universal Declaration on Human Duties and Responsibilities (1998):[8]

Article 1: "Every individual has duties towards himself, towards others, towards the family, towards the natural and cultural environment and towards the community, national and international, in which alone the free and full development of his personality is possible. He must exercise his rights and freedoms while being conscious that every right and freedom subsumes a corresponding duty."

Article 2: "While assuming the duties that are his, the individual must feel also fully responsible towards future generations preserving in particular the common heritage of mankind; he must always work for sustainable development and preserve biodiversity and the natural equilibrium, necessary to life and to the survival of humanity."

A further key aspect of CHM, that should not be overlooked, is its early articulation in the 1948

---

[7] Resolution 44 adopted on 12 November 1997 by the General Conference of UNESCO at its 29th Session (Paris).

[8] A copy of this draft declaration is appended to the article by Salvino Busuttil "Rights, Present Duties, Universal Responsibilities" in Salvino Busuttil and David Raphaël Busuttil (eds) *Telos Vol IV: What Future for Future Generations?* (Fondation de Malte, Valletta, 2010) 65-90.

draft World Constitution (Chicago Constitution).[9]
The first chapter is a declaration of *duties* and
rights (not solely rights), and provides:

"The four elements of life – earth, water, air,
energy – *are common property of the human race.
The management and use of* such portions thereof
as are vested in or assigned to particular ownership,
... *shall be subordinated in each and all cases to
the inherent interest of the common good."*
(emphasis added)

The group of eminent people who drafted
this document, including Elisabeth Mann Borgese,
her husband (Guiseppe Borgese) and her father
(Thomas Mann), were concerned that international
peace could only be attained if understood as being
connected to social and economic justice. This
could not be secured using existing concepts of
property, including the unfettered rights of use and
misuse and the absence of duties to protect and
share for the common good. Thus the draft
attempted to establish a new legal order to protect
the Earth and its resources as the common heritage
of mankind. In doing so, they drew not on
socialism but on Christian theology.[10]

---

[9] World Beyond Borders *Preliminary Draft of a World Constitution*
(1947-1948) available at www.worldbeyondborders.org/chicagodraft.
htm.
[10] Note however that there are many similarities between aspects of
Christian theology, that provide the conceptual framework of CHM, and

With this historical context of CHM in mind, together with its use as a core concept in the 'Constitution for the Oceans' (UNCLOS III), we can better appreciate its relevance and contribution to the great themes of our time – sustainable development, comprehensive security and collective management of the ecological commons.

This bibliography has been published by the Fondation de Malte. We are grateful for its support in seeing the project from inception to fruition and for taking on the task of its dissemination. It is absolutely appropriate that the Fondation de Malte publish this bibliography. CHM, as it has developed in legal literature, is very much due to the ongoing stewardship of the people of Malta and institutions located in that country.[11] It is a stewardship of which they are justifiably proud. We acknowledge the financial support of the University of Auckland, New Zealand.[12] We are also grateful

---

Eastern philosophy and spiritual traditions. See Elisabeth Mann Borgese "The Philosophy of the Common Heritage" in *The Future of the Oceans: A Report to the Club of Rome* (Harvest House, Montréal, 1986) 125. One of the best sources available, for appreciating the broader historical context of CHM, is Elisabeth Mann Borgese's Nexus Lecture "The Years of My Life" (2004) 18 Ocean Yearbook 1-21.

[11] In particular, the work of the International Ocean Institute (established by Elisabeth Mann Borgese) (http://www.ioinst.org) and the work of members of the IMO International Maritime Law Institute (http://www.imli.org).

[12] Some of the research for this bibliography was funded by the School of Architecture and Planning, University of Auckland. The authors also

for the kind assistance of the staff at the International Ocean Institute and at the Melitensia collection, University of Malta.

The task of editing this bibliography was complex and required a number of decisions to be made as we progressed. Some of these have been summarized in the following editorial comments. The purpose of these comments is to assist the user in understanding the parameters for the selection of work. It is our hope that this bibliography will serve as a tribute to all those people who have chosen to engage in scholarship on CHM and, that it will be a helpful research tool, for all those who choose to dive into its deep waters.

Prue Taylor[13] **and Lucy Stroud**[14]
September 2012
University of Auckland
New Zealand

---

acknowledge the support of the New Zealand Centre for Environmental Law (http://www.nzcel.auckland.ac.nz/uoa/).
[13] Prue Taylor, LLB, LLM (Hon), LLM (Envt'l & Energy), Senior Lecturer, School of Architecture and Planning, University of Auckland and Deputy Director, New Zealand Centre for Environmental Law (http://www.nzcel.auckland.ac.nz/uoa/) (Prue.Taylor@auckland.ac.nz).
[14] Lucy Stroud, LLB (Hon), Senior Researcher for the New Zealand Centre for Environmental Law, independent international law consultant and PhD Candidate in Law at the University of Auckland (lstroudnz@gmail.com).

EDITORIAL COMMENTS

1. Selection of Titles

This bibliography is merely a *starting point* for research on the Common Heritage of Mankind (CHM). Its primary focus is on academic legal writing, since 1967.

1.1. Key English words used to search databases:
- common heritage of mankind/humanity/humankind
- variations of the above terms such as humanity's heritage

1.2. Key foreign words used to search databases:
The words and meaning of the CHM in foreign languages can be difficult to decipher as they may convey disparate ideas. The search terms for CHM, in selected foreign languages and transliterations, were as follows:

- emberiség közös öröksége/nek
- gemeenschappelijk erfgoed der mensheid
- gemeinsame/n/er erbe der menschheit
- koinēs klēronomias tēs anorōpotētas
- obŝego nslediâ čelovečestva/obŝee nasledie čelovečestva
- patrimoine commun de l'humanité
- patrimônio comum da humanidade
- patrimonio común de la humanidad
- patrimonio comune dell'umanità
- skupna dediščina člověštva
- společnemu dědictvi lidstva

- wspólnego dziedzictwa ludzkości
- zajednička baština čovječanstva

The variations of these terms that were used encompass the following:

héritage commun de l'humanité, l'humanité de patrimoine commun, menschheitserbe, patrimoine culturel commun de l'humanité, patrimoine de l'humanité, patrimoine naturel de l'humanité, patrimonio comune della cultura, patrimonio cultural de la humanidad and patrimonio genetico dell'umanità.

A small facet of the hunt for CHM titles used the non-Latin scripts of Chinese, Greek and Cyrillic (such as the Russian phrases общее наследие человечества/общего наследия человечества and Serbian terms заједничко наслеђе човечанства).

1.3. Key words and terms excluded from database searches:

Titles that did not contain the above words or terms were excluded from the bibliography as well as titles that only alluded to the CHM with terms as illustrated below:

- areas/resources beyond the limits of national jurisdiction, Part XI of the United Nations Convention on the Law of the Sea [deep seabed provisions]

- common but differentiated responsibilities, common concern, common good, common interest (permitted one exception for authors Arvid Pardo and Carl Christol)

- common future, rights of future generations, common patrimony, inter-generational equity (with the exception of selected articles by Salvino Busuttil, Peter Serracino Inglott and Edith Brown Weiss)

- common pool resources, common resource, common spaces, commons concept, commons regime, global commons, ideology of the commons, public domain, public goods, res communis humanitatis, tragedy of the commons, space commons

- common law of mankind, law of common spaces

- global heritage, Grotius' heritage, patrimoine de l'espace, ressource patrimoniale

- mankind provisions/province of mankind [space law]

2. Translations

Titles composed in the following common languages were not translated: French, German, Italian, Portuguese and Spanish. However, we translated titles in the Latin script of Croatian, Czech, Dutch, Hungarian, Polish and Slovenian as well those in non-Latin scripts such as Chinese, Greek and Cyrillic (Russian, Serbian, Ukrainian).

3. Transliterations

To convert the titles composed in a non-Latin script, we employed several transliterations systems. ISO 9:1995 from the International Organization for Standardization was used for the transliteration into Latin characters of Cyrillic characters constituting the alphabets of Slavic and non-Slavic languages. To transliterate the original scripts, we pursued one-to-one mapping of characters into the Latin script with diacritics so that the transliteration is reversible (the exact reproduction of the original text may assist readers in locating cited materials). ISO 843 was used for the transliteration of Greek letters into Modern Greek, and the ALA-LC system availed the transliteration of Chinese characters into the Latin alphabet. Any errors in the transliterations and translations are the responsibility of the authors of this bibliography.

4. Sources

We compiled nearly 600 CHM titles that were sourced from 215 different journals, reviews, conference proceedings and magazines as well as from an array of books and presentations. These sources were primarily extracted from the myriad databases for legal literature, but they were also unearthed from academic fields interlinked with law such as the humanities (international relations, political studies, social sciences, philosophy and archaeology), business and economics, and science (biotechnology, environmental and marine).

The titles in this bibliography are elaborated with supplementary details (such as the different language versions of titles and source institutes) to assist the reader in locating the materials.

5. Selection of Subject Headings

The constellation and order of subject headings in the bibliography reflects the trajectory of CHM through diverse international debates, negotiations and laws.

6. Updating

Readers are invited to send any comments and suggestions they may have for updating this bibliography with new titles on the Common Heritage of Mankind to author Lucy Stroud (lstroudnz@gmail.com).

LIST OF CITED JOURNALS

1. Acta Astronautica
2. Acta Societatis Martensis
3. Acta Universitatis Lodziensis: Politologia
4. Actes
5. Actualité Juridique Droit Administratif
6. Agenda Internacional
7. American Journal of Economics and Sociology
8. American Journal of International Law
9. American University International Law Review
10. Annales: Anuario del Centro de la Universidad Nacional de Educación a Distancia de Barbastro
11. Annales d'Études Internationales = Annals of International Studies
12. Annals of Air and Space Law = Annales de Droit Aérien et Spatial
13. Annuaire de Droit Maritime et Aérien
14. Annuaire de Droit Maritime et Aéro-Spatial
15. Annuaire de Droit Maritime et Océanique
16. Anuario Argentino de Derecho Internacional
17. Anuario de Derecho Internacional
18. Anuario Hispano-Luso-Americano de Derecho Internacional
19. Archivio Giuridico Filippo Serafini
20. Ars Aequi
21. ASILS International Law Journal
22. Auckland University Law Review
23. Aus Politik und Zeitgeschichte
24. Beijing Da Xue Xue Bao = Journal of Peking University
25. Boletín Mexicano de Derecho Comparado
26. Boston College International and Comparative Law Review

119. McGill Law Journal
120. Manchester Journal of International Economic Law
121. Marine Technology Society Journal
122. Melbourne Journal of International Law
123. Michigan State Law Review
124. Millennium: Journal of International Studies
125. Mirovaâ Èkonomika i Meždunarodnye Otnošeniâ
126. Mondes en Développement
127. Mysore University Law Journal
128. Naturopa
129. Naval Law Review
130. Netherlands International Law Review
131. New Leader
132. New York University Journal of International Law and Politics
133. New Zealand Journal of Environmental Law
134. New Zealand Yearbook of International Law
135. Nord-Süd Aktuell: Vierteljahreszeitschrift für Nord-Süd und Süd-Süd Entwicklungen
136. NUJS Law Review
137. NZLawyer Magazine
138. Ocean and Coastal Management
139. Ocean Development and International Law
140. Ocean Management
141. Ocean Yearbook
142. Oceanus
143. Ottawa Law Review
144. Państwo i Prawo
145. Peace and the Sciences
146. Persona y Derecho
147. Polish Political Science Yearbook
148. Political and International Scientific and Research Quarterly
149. Právník: Teoretický Časopis pro Otázky Státu a Práva

1. CHM in the General Context

"A.C. Kiss reçoit le titre de docteur honoris causa et parle du patrimoine commun de l'humanité" (1983) 11(4) Environmental Policy and Law 92.

Anand, Ram Prakash "Equitable Use and Sharing of the Common Heritage of Mankind" in Alexander, Lewis M (ed) *Law of the Sea: Needs and Interests of Developing Countries: Proceedings of the Seventh Annual Conference of the Law of the Sea Institute, June 26–29, 1972, at the University of Rhode Island, Kingston, Rhode Island* (University of Rhode Island, Kingston, 1973) 70.
— "The Common Heritage of Mankind: Mutilation of an Ideal" (1997) 37(1) Indian Journal of International Law 1.
— "The Common Heritage of Mankind: Mutilation of an Ideal" in *Studies in International Law and History: An Asian Perspective* (Martinus Nijhoff Publishers, Leiden, 2004) 180.

Anderson, Stanley "Peaceful Dispute Resolution and a Common Heritage" (1982) 15(2) Center Magazine [Center for the Study of Democratic Institutions, Santa Barbara] 57.

Armas Barea, Calixto A "Patrimonio común de la humanidad: naturaleza jurídica, contenido normativo y prospectiva" (paper prepared for the 16th Congress of the Instituto Hispano-Luso-Americano de Derecho Internacional, Mérida (VE), 18–23 March 1991).
— "Los conceptos de 'interés de la humanidad' y 'patrimonio común de la humanidad'" in Armas Barea, Calixto A and Beltramino, Juan CM (eds) *Antártida al iniciarse la década de 1990: contribución al 30 aniversario de la entrada en vigencia del Tratado Antártico* (Ediciones Manantial, Buenos Aires, 1992) 19.
— "Patrimonio común de la humanidad: naturaleza jurídica, contenido normativo y prospectiva" (1993) 10 Anuario Hispano-Luso-Americano de Derecho Internacional 13.

Arnold, Rudolph P "The Common Heritage of Mankind as a Legal Concept" (1975) 9(1) International Lawyer 153.

Arzinger, Rainer "Legal Aspects of the Common Heritage of Mankind" in International Institute of Space Law of the International Astronautical Federation *Proceedings of the Twenty-Second Colloquium on the Law of Outer Space: September 16–22, 1979, Munich, Germany* (American Institute of Aeronautics and Astronautics, New York, 1980) 89.

Attard, Jérôme "Le fondement solidariste du concept 'environnement-patrimoine commun'" (2003) 2 Revue Juridique de l'Environnement 161.

Attfield, Robin "The Common Heritage of Mankind" in *Environmental Ethics: An Overview for the Twenty-First Century* (Polity Press, Cambridge (UK), 2003) 169.
— "Environmental Values, Nationalism, Global Citizenship and the Common Heritage of Humanity" in Lowe, Ian and Paavola, Jouni (eds) *Environmental Values in a Globalising World: Nature, Justice and Governance* (Routledge, London, 2005) 38.

Bardonnet, Daniel "Le projet de convention de 1912 sur le Spitsberg et le concept de patrimoine commun de l'humanité" in Dupuy, René-Jean and Ago, Roberto (eds) *Humanité et droit international: mélanges René-Jean Dupuy* (Éditions A. Pedone, Paris, 1991) 13.

Barsegov, Yuri G "Obŝee nasledie čelovečestva" [The Common Heritage of Mankind] in Andreev, E and others *Gornoe delo i okružaûŝaâ sreda: mirovoj opyt pravovoj garmonizacii* [Mining and the Environment: A World Perspective of Legal Harmonization] (Ministry of Defense, IASP, Moscow, 2000) 273. Russian.

Baslar, Kemal *The Concept of the Common Heritage of Mankind in International Law* (Martinus Nijhoff Publishers, The Hague, 1998).

Basso, Jacques "Le patrimoine de l'humanité" in United Nations Educational, Scientific and Cultural Organization *René-Jean Dupuy: une œuvre au service de l'humanité* (UNESCO, Paris, 1999) 101.

Bedjaoui, Mohammed "Contradictions in the Formulation of a New Legal Language: The Example of the Common Heritage of All Mankind" in *Towards a New International Economic Order* (UNESCO, Paris, 1979) 222.
— "Common Heritage or License to Exploit? A New World Economic Order: A Hard Look at its Meaning for International Law" (1979) 32(6) UNESCO Courier 12.
— "Are the World's Food Resources the Common Heritage of Mankind?" (1984) 24(4) Indian Journal of International Law 459.
— "Les denrées alimentaires de base, patrimoine commun de l'humanité". Communication au deuxième colloque international pour la réalisation du "Manifeste des Prix Nobel: pour des décisions immédiates contre la faim et le sous-développement et pour l'affirmation du droit à la vie et à la liberté", Chamber of Deputies, Rome, 14–15 February 1986.
— "Un possible 'patrimoine commun de l'humanité': les denrées alimentaires de base" (1986) 6 Survie: Journal de Food and Desarmament International 21.
— "Les ressources alimentaires essentielles en tant que 'patrimoine commun de l'humanité'" (1986) 1 Revue Algérienne des Relations Internationales 15.
— "Des œuvres de l'esprit d'intérêt universel comme patrimoine commun de l'humanité" in Vasak, Karel and Mayor, Federico (eds) *Karel Vasak amicorum liber: les droits de l'homme à l'aube du XXIe siècle = Los derechos humanos ante el siglo XXI = Human Rights at the Dawn of the Twenty-First Century* (Bruylant, Brussels, 1999) 951.

Bekkouche, Adda "La récupération du concept de patrimoine commun de l'humanité (PCH) par les pays industriels" (1987) 20(1) Revue Belge de Droit International = Belgian Review of International Law 124.

Belhaj, Fèrid "Que reste-t-il du concept de patrimoine commun de l'humanité?" (1990) 34 Études Internationales [Association des Études Internationales, Tunis] 83.

Bencheikh, Madjid "L'organisation institutionnelle du patrimoine commun de l'humanité" (1978) 15(4) Revue Algérienne des Sciences Juridiques, Èconomiques et Politiques 627.
— "Le patrimoine commun de l'humanité n'est pas organisé comme un instrument de lutte contre le sous-développement" in Bencheikh, Madjid; Charvin, Robert and Demichel, Francine *Introduction critique au droit international* (Presses Universitaires de Lyon, Lyon, 1986) 114.

Blanc Altemir, Antonio "El patrimonio común de la humanidad: ¿ un principio jurídico o simplemente una proposición ético-filosófica?" (1991–1992) 8–9 Annales: Anuario del Centro de la Universidad Nacional de Educación a Distancia de Barbastro 9.
— *El patrimonio común de la humanidad: hacia un régimen jurídico internacional para su gestión* (Editorial Bosch, Barcelona, 1992).

Bolintineanu, Alexandru "Le patrimoine commun de l'humanité et le droit de l'humanité" (1995) 6(2) Revue Roumaine de Sciences Juridiques 155.

Borg, Saviour F "The Common Heritage 1967–1997" in Rajagopalan, R (ed) *Common Heritage and the 21st Century: Proceedings of Pacem in Maribus XXV: November 1997* (International Ocean Institute in cooperation with the Foundation for International Studies and Government of Malta, Mside (MT), 1998) 83.

Boyce, James K "The Environment as Our Common Heritage" in *Economics, the Environment and Our Common Wealth* (Edward Elgar Publishing, Cheltenham, 2013) 1

Breidenbach, Joana and Nyíri, Pál "'Our Common Heritage': New Tourist Nations, Post-Socialist Pedagogy, and the Globalization of Nature" (2007) 48(2) Current Anthropology 322.

Brown, Edward D "The Common Heritage of Mankind as a Fundamental Principle – Ideology or Reality?" in *Sea-Bed Energy and Minerals: The International Legal Regime: Volume 2: Sea-Bed Mining* (Martinus Nijhoff Publishers, The Hague, 2001) 14.

Brown Weiss, Edith "International Law, Common Patrimony and Intergenerational Equity: Research in Progress" in Dupuy, René-Jean (ed) *L'avenir du droit international de l'environnement = The Future of the International Law of the Environment* (Workshop of the Hague Academy of International Law and United Nations University, The Hague, 12–14 November 1984; Martinus Nijhoff Publishers, Dordrecht, 1985) 445.
— *In Fairness to Future Generations: International Law, Common Patrimony, and Intergenerational Equity* (United Nations University, Tokyo, 1989).

Brownlie, Ian "Joint Exploitation of Resources and the Common Heritage of Mankind" (1979) 162 Recueil des Cours de l'Académie de Droit International de la Haye = Collected Courses of the Hague Academy of International Law 289.

Brunnée, Jutta "Common Areas, Common Heritage, Common Concern" in Bodansky, Daniel; Brunnée Jutta and Hey, Ellen (eds) *The Oxford Handbook of International Environmental Law* (Oxford University Press, Oxford, 2007) 551.

Brush, Stephen B "Is Common Heritage Outmoded?" in Brush, Stephen B and Stabinsky, Doreen (eds) *Valuing Local Knowledge: Indigenous People and Intellectual Property Rights* (Island Press, Washington (DC), 1996) 143.

Bueckling, Adrian "Zur juristischen substanzlosigkeit des begriffes: gemeinsames erbe der menschheit" (1981) 59 Deutsche Richterzeitung 288.
— "Der fluch der generalklauseln: vom treu- und glaubenssatz zum gemeinsamen erbe der menschheit" (1983) 16 Zeitschrift für Rechtspolitik 190.

Bula-Bula, Sayeman "Le patrimoine commun de l'humanité, institution du droit international moderne" in Yakpo, Emile and Boumedra, Tahar (eds) *Liber amicorum Judge Mohammed Bedjaoui* (Kluwer Law International, The Hague, 1999) 76.

Busuttil, Salvino "Protecting Our Common Future" in Agius, Emmanuel and Busuttil, Salvino (eds) *What Future for Future Generations? A Programme of UNESCO and the International Environment Institute* (Foundation for International Studies, University of Malta, Valletta, 1994) 151.
— "A Note on Future Generations in the Mediterranean" in Cortis, Toni; Freller, Thomas and Bugeja, Lino (eds) *Melitensium Amor: Festschrift in Honour of Dun Ġwann Azzoppardi* (Gutenberg Press, Malta, 2002) 409.

Carrillo Salcedo, Juan A "Le concept de patrimoine commun de l'humanité" in Société Française pour le Droit International (ed) *Ouvertures en droit international: hommage à René-Jean Dupuy* (Éditions A. Pedone, Paris, 2000) 55.

Chemillier-Gendreau, Monique "The Idea of the Common Heritage of Humankind and its Political Uses" (2002) 9(3) Constellations: An International Journal of Critical and Democratic Theory 375.

Christol, Carl Q "The Legal Common Heritage of Mankind: Capturing an Illusive Concept and Applying it to World Needs" in International Institute of Space Law of the International Astronautical Federation *Proceedings of the Eighteenth Colloquium on the Law of Outer Space:*

September 21–27, 1975, Lisbon, Portugal (University of California School of Law, Davis, 1976) 42.

— "Implementation of the Common Heritage Principle" (paper presented to the 70th Conference of the International Law Association, Space Law Committee, New Delhi, 2–6 April 2002).

Ciciriello, Maria C "The Principle of the Common Heritage of Mankind and its Application in Contemporary International Law: Results of a Research" (1989) 2 Yearbook of the University of Rome II, Department of Public Law 609.

— "Dal principio del patrimonio comune al concetto di sviluppo sostenibile" in Comitato nazionale per la celebrazione del 50 anniversario dell'ONU, Società Italiana per l'Organizzazione Internazionale (SIOI) *L'ONU: cinquant'anni di attività e prospettive per il futuro. Atti dei convegni organizzati dalla SIOI a Torino, Bologna, Palermo, Napoli e Bari in occasione della celebrazione del 50 anniversario dell'ONU* (SIOI, Rome, 1996) 265. Reprinted in (1996) 5(4) Diritto e Giurisprudenza Agraria e dell'Ambiente 225.

Club des Relations Internationales *Le patrimoine commun de l'humanité, illusion ou espoir de survie? XVe congrès annuel du Club de Relations Internationales, 12 et 13 mars 1982, Université de Montréal* (CRI, Montréal, 1982).

Cocca, Aldo A "Antecedentes y desarrollo de la doctrina Argentina del patrimonio común de la humanidad en el moderno derecho internacional" in Pérez Montero, José (ed) *Liber amicorum: colección de estudios jurídicos en homenaje al Prof. Dr. D. José Pérez Montero* (Universidad de Oviedo Servicio de Publicaciones, Oviedo (ES), 1988) vol 1, 325.

— "Common Heritage of Mankind: A Basic Principle of the International Legal System" in International Institute of Space Law of the International Astronautical Federation *Proceedings of the Thirty-First Colloquium on the Law of Outer Space: October 8–14, 1988, Bangalore, India*

(American Institute of Aeronautics and Astronautics, Reston, 1989) 89.
— "Environment as a Common Heritage of Mankind" in International Institute of Space Law of the International Astronautical Federation *Proceedings of the Thirty-Second Colloquium on the Law of Outer Space: October 11–15, 1989, Torremolinos-Málaga, Spain* (American Institute of Aeronautics and Astronautics, Reston, 1990) 71.

Cooper, Richard N "Common Heritage" in *Environment and Resource Policies for the World Economy* (Brookings Institution Press, Washington (DC), 1994) 11.

Coquia, Jorge R "The Common Heritage of Mankind: A New Hope of Developing States" (1988) 3(4) Foreign Relations Journal 17.

Corriente Córdoba, José A "Globalización, intereses y patrimonio de la humanidad y patrimonio mundial" in Drnas de Clément, Zlata (ed) *Estudios de derecho internacional en homenaje al Profesor Ernesto J. Rey Caro* (Drnas-Lerner Editores, Córdoba (AR), 2002) vol 1, 259.
— "Globalización, patrimonio de la humanidad y patrimonio mundial" in Peláez Marón, José M (ed) *Globalización, deuda externa y exigencias de justicia social* (Ediciones AKAL, Madrid, 2003) 57.

Daillier, Patrick "Tiers monde et 'patrimoine commun de l'humanité'" (1983) 273 Économie et Humanisme 50.

Danilenko, Gennady M "The Concept of the 'Common Heritage of Mankind' in International Law" (1988) 13 Annals of Air and Space Law = Annales de Droit Aérien et Spatial 247.

Das, Rukmini "Compensation as Equity in Context of Common Heritage of Mankind: A Key to Sustainability and Inter-Generational & Inter-Regional Equity" (2009) 2(2) NUJS Law Review 267.

de Klemm, Cyrille "Le patrimoine naturel de l'humanité" in Dupuy, René-Jean (ed) *L'avenir du droit international de l'environnement = The Future of the International Law of the Environment* (Workshop of the Hague Academy of International Law and United Nations University, The Hague, 12–14 November 1984; Martinus Nijhoff Publishers, Dordrecht, 1985) 117.

Dekanozov, Reginald V "Ponâtie 'obŝego nslediâ čelovečestva' v meždunarodnom prave" [The Notion of 'Common Heritage of Mankind' in International Law] (1981) Sovetskij Ežegodnik Meždunarodnogo Prava [Soviet Yearbook of International Law] 142. Russian with summary in English.
— "Forming of the Principle of the Common Heritage of Mankind and the Rules of Customary International Law" in International Institute of Space Law of the International Astronautical Federation *Proceedings of the Twenty-Fifth Colloquium on the Law of Outer Space: September 27– October 2, 1982, Paris, France* (American Institute of Aeronautics and Astronautics, New York, 1983) 215.

Deng, Achol "Natural Resources: Heritage of Nation and Mankind" in Grahl-Madsen, Atle and Toman, Jiri (eds) *The Spirit of Uppsala: Proceedings of the Joint UNITAR-Uppsala University Seminar on International Law and Organization for a New World Order (JUS 81), Uppsala, 9–18 June 1981* (Walter De Gruyter, Berlin, 1984) 308.

Dingli, Sandra M "A Plea for Responsibility Towards the Common Heritage of Mankind" in Scarre, Christopher and Scarre, Geoffrey (eds) *The Ethics of Archaeology: Philosophical Perspectives on Archaeological Practice* (Cambridge University Press, Cambridge, 2006) 219.

Dolman, Anthony J "The Common Heritage of Mankind and Global Reform" in *Resources, Regimes, World Order* (Pergamon Press, New York, 1981) 223.

Dolzer, Rudolf "The Global Environmental Facility – Towards a New Concept of the Common Heritage of Mankind?" in Alfredsson, Gudmundur and Macalister-Smith, Peter (eds) *The Living Law of Nations: Essays on Refugees, Minorities, Indigenous Peoples, and the Human Rights of Other Vulnerable Groups: In Memory of Atle Grahl-Madsen* (NP Engel, Arlington (US), 1996) 331.

Doyle, Stephen E "Legal and Policy Implications of Treating Natural Resources as the Common Heritage of Mankind" in International Institute of Space Law of the International Astronautical Federation *Proceedings of the Twenty-Ninth Colloquium on the Law of Outer Space: October 4–11, 1986, Innsbruck, Austria* (American Institute of Aeronautics and Astronautics, New York, 1987) 31.

Driscoll Sullivan, Colleen "The Common Heritage Institute's 20th Anniversary Colloquium on 'The Common Heritage Concept: Past, Present and Future', Villanova, December 11 and 12 1987" (1988) 16(1) Journal of Space Law 88.

Drzewicki, Krzysztof "Idea wspólnego dziedzictwa ludzkości a prawa człowieka" [The Idea of the Common Heritage of Mankind and Human Rights] (1982) 1–3 Przegląd Stosunków Międzynarodowych [International Affairs Review] 47. Polish.

Dupuy, René-Jean "L'héritage commun de l'humanité pour le développement" in *L'océan partagé: analyse d'une négociation (troisiéme conférence des nations unies sur le droit de la mer)* (Éditions A. Pedone, Paris, 1979) 141.
— "Réflexions sur le patrimoine commun de l'humanité" (1985) 1 Droits: Revue Française de Théorie Juridique 63.
— "Réflexions sur le patrimoine commun de l'humanité" (1986) 364(4) Études: Revue Fondée en 1856 par des Pères de la Compagnie de Jésus 489.

Dutfield, Graham "Sovereignty, Common Heritage and Property Rights" in *Intellectual Property, Biogenetic*

Resources and Traditional Knowledge (Earthscan, London, 2004) 3.

Eberlee, John "Our Common Heritage: Some Areas of the Globe and All of the Universe Are Not the Sovereign Territory of Any Nation" (1990) 55(7) Canada and the World 24.

Fenech-Adami, Edward "The Common Heritage of Mankind: A Linking Concept Between Christian Democracy and Global Ecology" in Philipp, Jenninger (ed) *Unverdrossen für Europa: festschrift für Kai-Uwe von Hassel zum 75. geburtstag* (Nomos, Baden-Baden (DE), 1988) 177.

Fitschen, Thomas "Gemeinsames erbe der menschheit" in Wolfrum, Rüdiger (ed) *Handbuch der Vereinten Nationen* (2nd revised ed, CH Beck, Munich, 1991) 211.
— "Common Heritage of Mankind" in Wolfrum, Rüdiger and Philipp, Christiane (eds) *United Nations: Law, Policies and Practice* (Martinus Nijhoff Publishers, Munich, 1995) vol 1, 149.

Fitzmaurice, Malgosia A [Part I:] "Common Heritage of Mankind (CHM)" (2001) 293 Recueil des Cours de l'Académie de Droit International de la Haye = Collected Courses of the Hague Academy of International Law 150.

Fleischer, Carl A "The International Concern for the Environment: The Common Heritage of Mankind" in Bothe, Michael (ed) *Trends in Environmental Policy and Law = Tendances actuelles de la politique et du droit de l'environnement* (International Union for Conservation of Nature and Natural Resources, Gland (CH), 1980) 321.

Flory, Maurice "Le patrimoine commun de l'humanité dans le droit international de l'environnement" in Chérot, Jean-Yves *Droit et environnement: propos pluridisciplinaires sur un droit en construction* (Presses Universitaires d'Aix-Marseille, Aix-en-Provence, 1995) 39.

Frankman, Myron J "Fractals and the Common Heritage of Humanity" (paper presented to the 9th Annual Conference of the Canadian Association for the Study of International Development, Ottawa, 9 June 1993).
— "From the Common Heritage Principle to a Planet-Wide Citizen's Income" (2001) 2 McGill International Review 14.
— "From the Common Heritage of Mankind to a Planet-Wide Citizen's Income: Establishing the Basis for Solidarity" (paper presented to the Conference From Vancouver to Vladivostok: University Voluntarism for a Participative Society, Santander (ES), 29 June 2001).

French, Hillary "Preserving the Common Heritage" in *After the Earth Summit: The Future of Environmental Governance* (WorldWatch Institute, Washington (DC), 1992) 8.

Fu, Kuen-Chen "Common Heritage of Mankind – Opportunities of Taiwan to Share" (1983) 12(1) Guo Li Taiwan Da Xue Fa Xue Lun Cong [National Taiwan University Law Journal] 114.

Fuse, Tsutomu "Common Heritage of Mankind in 21st Century" in Rajagopalan, R (ed) *Common Heritage and the 21st Century: Proceedings of Pacem in Maribus XXV: November 1997* (International Ocean Institute in cooperation with the Foundation for International Studies and Government of Malta, Mside (MT), 1998) 92.

Gadkowski, Tadeusz "Prawo do wspólnego dziedzictwa ludzkości" [The Right to the Common Heritage of Mankind] in Polska Akademia Nauk, Instytut Nauk Prawnych [Polish Academy of Sciences, Institute of Legal Studies] *Prawa człowieka: model prawny* [Human Rights: Legal Model] (Zakład Narodowy imienia Ossolińskich – Wydawnictwo, Wrocław (PL), 1991) 53. Polish.

Galloway, Jonathan F "Political Philosophy and the Common Heritage of Mankind Concept in International Law" in International Institute of Space Law of the

International Astronautical Federation *Proceedings of the Twenty-Third Colloquium on the Law of Outer Space: September 21–28, 1980, Tokyo, Japan* (American Institute of Aeronautics and Astronautics, New York, 1981) 25.

— "Globalization, Sovereignty and the Common Heritage" in International Institute of Space Law of the International Astronautical Federation *Proceedings of the Forty-Second Colloquium on the Law of Outer Space: October 4–8, 1999, Amsterdam, The Netherlands* (American Institute of Aeronautics and Astronautics, Reston, 2000) 340.

Gangale, Thomas "Common Heritage in Magnificent Desolation" (paper presented to the 46th American Institute of Aeronautics and Astronautics (AIAA) Aerospace Sciences Meeting, Reno, 7–10 January 2008).

Garrison, Christopher "Beneath the Surface: The Common Heritage of Mankind" (2007) 1 Knowledge Ecology Studies 1 <http://www.kestudies.org>.

Gattini, Andrea *Il common heritage of mankind: una rivoluzione in diritto internazionale?* (A. Giuffrè Editore, Milan, 1985).

Gaurier, Dominique and Hesse, Philippe-Jean "La permanence d'un mythe: patrimoine commun des pauvres ou patrimoine commun de l'humanité?" (1991) 11 Annuaire de Droit Maritime et Aéro-Spatial 61.

Ge, Yong-Ping "Study on the Relation Between the Principle of 'Common Heritage of Mankind' and the Other Relative Principles" (2007) 11 Hebei Fa Xue = Hebei Law Science Journal 119. Chinese.

Goldie, Louis FE "A Note on Some Diverse Meanings of 'The Common Heritage of Mankind'" (1983) 10(1) Syracuse Journal of International Law and Commerce 69.

Goldwin, Robert A "Common Sense vs. 'Common Heritage'" in Oxman, Bernard H; Caron, David D and

Buderi, Charles LO (eds) *Law of the Sea: U.S. Policy Dilemma* (Institute for Contemporary Studies Press, San Francisco, 1983) 59.

Gómez Isa, Felipe "Patrimonio común de la humanidad" (1993) 41(2) Estudios de Deusto: Revista de la Universidad de Deusto 119.

Gorove, Stephen "The Concept of 'Common Heritage of Mankind': A Political, Moral or Legal Innovation?" (1972) 9(3) San Diego Law Review 390.
— "The Concept of 'Common Heritage'" in *Studies in Space Law: Its Challenges and Prospects* (AW Sitjhoff, Leiden, 1977) 65.

Grimaud, Marie-Angéle; Hilling, Carol and Bernardi, Marie-Josée *Le concept de patrimoine commun de l'humanité* (report prepared for the Centre de Recherche en Droit Public de l'Université de Montréal, Montréal, 1997).

Gros Espiell, Héctor "El derecho de todos los seres humanos a beneficiarse del patrimonio común de la humanidad" (paper presented to the UNESCO Symposium on the Study of New Human Rights: The Rights of Solidarity, Mexico City, 12–15 August 1980).
— "El derecho de todos los seres humanos a beneficiarse de patrimonio común de la humanidad" in *Estudios sobre derechos humanos* (Ediciones del Instituto Interamericano de los Derechos Humanos, Caracas, 1985) 137.

Groulier, Cédric "Quelle effectivité juridique pour le concept de patrimoine commun?" (2005) 19 Actualité Juridique Droit Administratif 1034.

Haight, George W "Comments on Judge Oda's Approach to the Common Heritage of Mankind" (1981) 3(1) Journal of International and Comparative Law 15.

Heits, HF "El hombre debe respetar lo que integra el patrimonio común de la humanidad" (1987) 51(129) La Ley

Actualidad (Buenos Aires) 1 [summarizing an address by Nagendra Singh, President of the International Court of Justice].

Herrera Cáceres, H Roberto *En defensa del 'patrimonio común de la humanidad'* (Universidad Nacional Autonóma de Honduras, Tegucigalpa, 1982).
— "La sauvegarde du patrimoine commun de l'humanité" in Dupuy, René-Jean (ed) *La gestion des ressources pour l'humanité: le droit de la mer = The Management of Humanity's Resources: The Law of the Sea* (Workshop of the Hague Academy of International Law and United Nations University, The Hague, 29–31 October 1981; Martinus Nijhoff Publishers, The Hague, 1982) 125.

Hobe, Stephan "Was bleibt vom gemeinsamen erbe der menschheit?" in Dicke, Klaus and others (eds) *Weltinnenrecht: liber amicorum Jost Delbrück* (Duncker and Humbolt, Berlin, 2005) 329.

Hossain, Kamal "Natural Resources: Heritage of Nation and Mankind" in Grahl-Madsen, Atle and Toman, Jiri (eds) *The Spirit of Uppsala: Proceedings of the Joint UNITAR-Uppsala University Seminar on International Law and Organization for a New World Order (JUS 81), Uppsala, 9–18 June 1981* (Walter De Gruyter, Berlin, 1984) 302.

Höver, Gerhard "Solidarität und entwicklung. Zur bedeutung der menschenrechte im hinblick auf das 'gemeinsame erbe der menschheit'" in Hunold, Gerfried W and Korff, Wilhelm (eds) *Die welt für morgen: ethische herausforderungen im anspruch der zukunft* (Kösel-Verlag, Munich, 1986) 142.

Hudson, Richard "The Common Heritage of Mankind" (1976) 9(6) Ceres [Food and Agriculture Organization of the United Nations] 18.

Imnadze, Levan B "Common Heritage of Mankind: A Concept of Cooperation in Our Interdependent World?" in

Kuribayshi, Tadao and Miles, Edward L (eds) *The Law of the Sea in the 1990s: A Framework for Further International Cooperation: Proceedings, The Law of the Sea Institute Twenty-Fourth Annual Conference, July 24–27, 1990, Tokyo, Japan* (Law of the Sea Institute, University of Hawaii, Honolulu, 1992) 312.

Jagels-Sprenger, Monika "'Common heritage of mankind': vom internationalen nutzungs-und verteilungsregime zur herausbildung einer bewirtschaftungsordnung zum schutz der natürlichen ressourcen" (1991) 24(4) Kritische Justiz: Vierteljahresschrift für Recht und Politik 409.
— *Der grundsatz 'gemeinsames erbe der menschheit' im internationalen vertragsrecht zum schutz der natürlichen ressourcen* (Zentrum für Europäische Rechtspolitik an der Universität Bremen, Bremen, 1991).

Jamali, Hmaidreza "A Critical Examination of Historical Theory of Sovereignty in the Light of Common Heritage of Mankind" (2009) 1(3) Political and International Scientific and Research Quarterly 101 <www.sid.ir>. Persian with abstract in English.
— "The International Environment and Common Heritage of Mankind" (2010) 2(4) Political and International Scientific and Research Quarterly 119 <www.sid.ir>. Persian with abstract in English.

Johnston, James L "The Economics of the Common Heritage of Mankind" (1979) 13 Marine Technology Society Journal 26.

Joyner, Christopher C "Legal Implications of the Concept of the Common Heritage of Mankind" (1986) 35(1) International and Comparative Law Quarterly 190.

Kahn, Philippe "Les patrimoines communs de l'humanité: quelques réflexions" in Prieur, Michel and Lambrechts, Claude (eds) *Les hommes et l'environnement: quels droits pour le vingt-et-unième siècle? Études en hommage à Alexandre Kiss = Mankind and the Environment: What*

Rights for the Twenty-First Century? Studies in Honour of Alexandre Kiss (Éditions Frison-Roche, Paris, 1998) 307.

Kalland, Arne "Nature: The Common Heritage of Mankind?" (paper presented to the 1st Performing Nature Workshop, University of Oslo, Oslo, 29–31 August 2007).

Kamto, Maurice "Les forêts, 'patrimoine commun de l'humanité' et droit international" in Prieur, Michel and Doumbé-Billé, Stéphane (eds) *Droit, forêts et développement durable: actes des 1ères journées scientifiques du réseau 'droit de l'environnement' de l'AUPELF-UREF á Limoges, 7–8 novembre 1994* (Bruylant, Brussels, 1996) 79.

Keats, Derek W and Shuttleworth, Mark "Toward a View of Knowledge as the Common Heritage of Humanity: Mapping an Open Content Strategy" in Beebe, Maria A and others (eds) *Africa Dot Edu: IT Opportunities and Higher Education in Africa* (Tata McGraw-Hill, New York, 2003).

Keles, Rusen "The Common Heritage of Mankind and the New Concepts of Responsibility" in Vlavianos-Arvanitis, Agni and Morovic, Jan (eds) *Biopolitics – The Bio-Environment, Volume VI: Danube River Bonds* (Proceedings of the 7th Annual Conference of the Biopolitics International Organization on Danube River Bonds: Bio-Environment and Bio-Culture, Bratislava, 3–6 June 1997; Biopolitics International Organization, Athens, 1998) 412.

Kewenig, Wilhelm A "Common heritage of mankind – politischer slogan oder völkerrechtlicher schlüsselbegriff?" in von Münch, Ingo (ed) *Staatsrecht – völkerrecht – europarecht. Festschrift für Hans-Jürgen Schlochauer zum 75. geburtstag am 28 märz 1981* (Walter de Gruyter, Berlin, 1981) 385.
— "Common Heritage of Mankind – A Political Slogan or a Key Concept of International Law?" (1981) 24 Law and State 7.

— "Menschheitserbe, konsens und völkerrechtsordnung" (1981) 36 Europa-Archiv: Zeitschrift für Internationale Politik 1.

Kiss, Alexandre C "La notion de patrimoine commun de l'humanité" (1982) 175 Recueil des Cours de l'Académie de Droit International de la Haye = Collected Courses of the Hague Academy of International Law 99.
— "The Common Heritage Principle: Utopia or Reality?" (1985) 40(3) International Journal [Canadian Institute of International Affairs] 423.
— "Conserving the Common Heritage of Mankind" (1990) 59(4) Revista Jurídica Universidad de Puerto Rico 773.
— "Nature, the Common Heritage of Humankind" (1999) 91 Naturopa 10.
— "The Common Heritage Principle: Utopia or Reality?" in Caminos, Hugo (ed) *Law of the Sea* (Ashgate/Dartmouth Publishing, Aldershot (UK), 2001) 323.
— "Nature, Our Common Heritage" in *Nature as Heritage: From Awareness to Action: Proceedings: Strasbourg (France), 3-4 June 1999* (Council of Europe Publishing, Strasbourg, 2002) 5.
— "The Common Heritage Principle: Utopia or Reality?" in De Feyter, Koen (ed) *Globalization and Common Responsibilities of States* (Ashgate Publishing, Farnham (UK), 2013) 89.

Klimenko, Boris M *Obšee nasledie čelovečestva: meždunarodno-pravovye voprosy* [The Common Heritage of Mankind: International Law Issues] (Izd-vo Instituta Meždunarodnye Otnošeniâ, Moscow, 1989). Russian.

Koester, Veit "A Common Heritage" (1981) 39 Naturopa 15.

Kolk, Gregor "Common Heritage of Mankind" in Volger, Helmut (ed) *A Concise Encyclopedia of the United Nations* (2nd revised ed, Martinus Nijhoff Publishers, Leiden, 2010) 47.

Kolodkin, Anatoly L "Princip obŝego naslediâ čelovečestva" [The Principle of Common Heritage of Mankind] in Movchan, Anatoly P and Yankov, Alexander (eds) *Mirovoj okean i meždunarodnoe pravo: osnovy sovremennogo pravoporâdka v mirovom okeane* [World Ocean and International Law: Foundations of Modern Law and Order in the World's Oceans] (Nauka, Moscow, 1986) 258. Russian.

Koroma, Abdul "The Future of the Common Heritage of Mankind" in Oxman, Bernard H and Koers, Albert W (eds) *The 1982 Convention on the Law of the Sea: Proceedings, Law of the Sea Institute Seventeenth Annual Conference, July 13–16, 1983, Oslo, Norway* (Law of the Sea Institute, University of Hawaii, Honolulu, 1984) 24.

Kouassi, Kanga "Le concept du patrimoine commun de l'humanité et l'évolution du droit international public" (1985) 39(3–4) Revue Juridique et Politique: Indépendance et Coopération 949.

Krieger, David "Linking Our Common Heritage With Our Common Future" in Mann Borgese, Elisabeth (ed) *Peace in the Oceans: Ocean Governance and the Agenda for Peace: Proceedings of Pacem in Maribus XXIII: Costa Rica, 3–7 December 1995* (UNESCO, Paris, 1997) 73.

Kullenberg, Gunnar and Holland, Geoffrey L "Environmental and Biodiversity Aspects: The Common Heritage of All Living Beings" in Rajagopalan, R (ed) *Common Heritage and the 21st Century: Proceedings of Pacem in Maribus XXV: November 1997* (International Ocean Institute in cooperation with the Foundation for International Studies and Government of Malta, Mside (MT), 1998) 109.

Kuppuswamy, Chamundeeswari "The Common Heritage of Mankind (CHM) and Intellectual Property Rights (IPR)" in *The International Legal Governance of the Human Genome* (Routledge, London, 2009) 134.

— "The Common Heritage of Mankind (CHM) in International Law" in *The International Legal Governance of the Human Genome* (Routledge, London, 2009) 49.
— "The Common Heritage of Mankind (CHM) and the Right to Development (RTD)" in *The International Legal Governance of the Human Genome* (Routledge, London, 2009) 80.
— "Human Rights, Common Heritage and Development" in *The International Legal Governance of the Human Genome* (Routledge, London, 2009) 107.

Larschan, Bradley and Brennan, Bonnie C "The Common Heritage of Mankind Principle in International Law" (1983) 21(2) Columbia Journal of Transnational Law 305.

Leary, David K "The Common Heritage of Mankind" in *International Law and the Genetic Resources of the Deep Sea* (Martinus Nijhoff Publishers, Leiden, 2007) 95.

Legault, Leonard H "Some Comments on the Concept of the Common Heritage of Mankind" in Canadian Council on International Law = Conseil Canadien de Droit International (ed) *International Regulation and Deregulation: Emerging Trends in the Role of International Institutions: Proceedings: XIV Annual Conference: October 17–19, 1985, Ottawa, Ontario = Réglementation et déréglementation internationale: évolution du rôle des institutions internationales: travaux: 17–19 octobre 1985, Ottawa, Ontario* (Canadian Council on International Law, Ottawa, 1986) 243.

Liang, Shuying "The Implication of the Principle of the Common Heritage of Mankind" (1990) 35(5) Zheng Fa Lun Tan: Zhongguo Zheng Fa Da Xue Xue Bao [Journal of China University of Political Science and Law] 44. Chinese.

Lissner, Will "Mankind's Common Heritage" (1978) 37(1) American Journal of Economics and Sociology 68.

Lodge, Michael W "The Common Heritage of Mankind" (2012) 27(4) International Journal of Marine and Coastal Law 733.

— "Implementation of the Common Heritage of Mankind" in Scheiber, Harry N and Paik, Jin-Hyun (eds) *Regions, Institutions, and Law of the Sea: Studies in Ocean Governance* (Martinus Nijhoff Publishers, Leiden, 2013) 129.

— "The Common Heritage of Mankind" in Freestone, David (ed) *The 1982 Law of the Sea Convention at 30: Successes, Challenges and New Agendas* (Martinus Nijhoff Publishers, Leiden, 2013) 59.

López Zamarripa, Norka "Régimen legal internacional en torno del patrimonio común de la humanidad" (2001) 4 Derecho y Cultura [Academia Mexicana para el Derecho, la Educación y la Cultura] 121.

Macdonald, Ronald StJ "The Common Heritage of Mankind" in Beyerlin, Ulrich and others (eds) *Recht zwischen umbruch und bewahrung: völkerrecht, europarecht, staatsrecht: festschrift für Rudolf Bernhardt* (Springer, Berlin, 1995) 153.

Maduka, Chikezie C *International Information Relations in the New Millennium: Interrelationship with the Common Heritage of Mankind* (Xlibris, Bloomington (US), 2000).

Magdelénat, Jean-Louis "The Common Heritage of Mankind" in Canadian Council on International Law = Conseil Canadien de Droit International (ed) *International Regulation and Deregulation: Emerging Trends in the Role of International Institutions: Proceedings: XIV Annual Conference: October 17–19, 1985, Ottawa, Ontario = Réglementation et déréglementation internationale: évolution du rôle des institutions internationales: travaux: 17–19 octobre 1985, Ottawa, Ontario* (Canadian Council on International Law, Ottawa, 1986) 259.

Mahiou, Ahmed "L'Afrique et le patrimoine commun de l'humanité" (1988) 3 Espaces et Ressources Maritimes 1.
— "Les espaces internationaux: entre hégémonie étatique et patrimoine commun de l'humanité" (2009) 337 Recueil des Cours de l'Académie de Droit International de la Haye = Collected Courses of the Hague Academy of International Law 474.

Mahmoudi, Said "Common Heritage of Mankind, Common Concern of Humanity" in Beurier, Jean-Pierre; Kiss, Alexandre C and Mahmoudi, Said (eds) *New Technologies and Law of the Marine Environment = Nouvelles technologies et droit de l'environnement marin* (Kluwer Law International, The Hague, 2000) 215.

Malenovský, Jiří "Od 'res communis omnium' ke 'společnemu dědictvi lidstva'?" [From 'res communis omnium' to a 'Common Heritage of Mankind?'] (1978) 117(6) Právnik: Teoretický Časopis pro Otázky Státu a Práva [The Lawyer – Scientific Review for Problems of State and Law] 558. Czech.

Malkassian, Roberto M "Contenido del principio de patrimonio común de la humanidad en el derecho internacional positivo" (1984–1986) 2 Anuario Argentino de Derecho Internacional 277.

Mann Borgese, Elisabeth "The Common Heritage: Only when Satellite Detection of Natural Resources is Governed by International Law Will it Benefit Mankind" (1974) 7(6) Ceres [Food and Agriculture Organization of the United Nations] 55.
— "The Common Heritage of Mankind" (Inter-Documentation, Zug (CH), 1975). Microfiche (RIO-1976, No. 1207).
— "Expanding the Common Heritage of Mankind" in Dolman, Anthony J (ed) *Global Planning and Resource Management: Toward International Decision-Making in a Divided World* (Pergamon Press, New York, 1980) 181.

— "The Economics of the Common Heritage" in *The Future of the Oceans: A Report to the Club of Rome* (Harvest House, Montréal, 1986) 43.

— "The Philosophy of the Common Heritage" in *The Future of the Oceans: A Report to the Club of Rome* (Harvest House, Montréal, 1986) 125.

— "The Common Heritage of Mankind for the Twenty-First Century" in Friggieri, Joe and Busuttil, Salvino (eds) *Interfaces – Essays in Philosophy and Bordering Areas in Honour of Peter Serracino Inglott* (University of Malta, Msida, 1997) 189.

— "The Economics of the Common Heritage" (2000) 43(8–9) Ocean and Coastal Management 763.

— "The Common Heritage of Mankind: From Non-Living Resources to Living Resources and Beyond" in Ando, Nisuke; McWhinney, Edward and Wolfrum, Rüdiger (eds) *Liber amicorum Judge Shigeru Oda* (Kluwer Law International, The Hague, 2002) vol 2, 1313.

Massulam, Lewis "The Common Heritage of Mankind: Success or Failure of International Regulation?" in Canadian Council on International Law = Conseil Canadien de Droit International (ed) *International Regulation and Deregulation: Emerging Trends in the Role of International Institutions: Proceedings: XIV Annual Conference: October 17–19, 1985, Ottawa, Ontario = Réglementation et déréglementation internationale: évolution du rôle des institutions internationales: travaux: 17–19 octobre 1985, Ottawa, Ontario* (Canadian Council on International Law, Ottawa, 1986) 248.

Mavi, Viktor "Az emberiség közös örökségének elve a mai nemzetközi jogban: jogszabály avagy filozófia?" [The Principle of Common Heritage of Mankind in Modern International Law: Norm or Philosophy?] (1985) 40(12) Jogtudományi Közlöny [Journal of Jurisprudence] 673. Hungarian.

Mercure, Pierre-François "L'échec des modèles de gestion des ressources naturelles selon les caractéristiques du

concept de patrimoine commun de l'humanité" (1996) 28(1) Ottawa Law Review 45.
— "La proposition d'un modéle de gestion intégréé des ressources naturelles communes de l'humanité" (1998) 36 Canadian Yearbook of International Law = Annuaire Canadien de Droit International 41.

Mickelson, Karin "Co-opting Common Heritage: Reflections on the Need for South-North Scholarship" in Okafor, Obiora C and Aginam, Obijiofor (eds) *Humanizing Our Global Order: Essays in Honour of Ivan Head* (University of Toronto Press, Toronto, 2003) 112.

Milić, Milenko *Common Heritage of Mankind: Working Paper of the World Peace Through Law Center* (World Peace Through Law Center, Washington (DC), 1975).

Milovanović, Zlatibor "What Does the Common Heritage of Mankind Mean?" in Logue, John J (ed) *Peace, Justice and the Law of the Sea: The Proceedings of a Villanova Colloquium in Honor of Dr. Arvid Pardo to Mark the Tenth Anniversary of his November 1, 1967 Address to the United Nations General Assembly* (World Order Research Institute, Villanova University, Villanova (US), 1978) 1.

Myers, David S "Is there a 'Common Heritage of Mankind?'" in International Institute of Space Law of the International Astronautical Federation *Proceedings of the Thirty-Third Colloquium on the Law of Outer Space: October 6–12, 1990, Dresden, Germany* (American Institute of Aeronautics and Astronautics, Reston, 1991) 335.

Nacib, A "L'humanité et la notion de patrimoine commun" (1996) 4 Revue Algérienne des Sciences Juridiques, Èconomiques et Politiques 724. Arabic.

Nagy, Boldizsár "Common Heritage of Mankind: The Status of Future Generations" in International Institute of Space Law of the International Astronautical Federation *Proceedings of the Thirty-First Colloquium on the Law of*

Outer Space: October 8–14, 1988, Bangalore, India (American Institute of Aeronautics and Astronautics, Reston, 1989) 319.

— "Common Heritage of Humanity: Status of Future Generations" (1990) 1 Future Generations Journal 4.

— "Az emberiség közös öröksége: a rejtőzködő jogosított" [The Common Heritage of Humanity: The Elusive Subject] in Bokorné Szegő, Hanna (ed) *Az államok nemzetközi közösségének változása és a nemzetközi jog* [International Law and Changes in the International Community of States] (Akadémiai Könyvkiadó, Budapest, 1993) 113. Hungarian.

— "Az emberiség közös öröksége és a jövő nemzedékek érdekei" [The Common Heritage of Humanity and the Interests of Future Generations] (lecture to the University of Debrecen, Debrecen (HU), 18 May 2005).

Nanda, Ved P and Pring, George W "Common Heritage of Humankind – The 'Global Commons'" in *International Environmental Law and Policy for the 21st Century* (Transnational Publishers, Ardsley, 2004) 33.

Nathan, Ari "Defining the 'Common Heritage of Mankind'" in Susskind, Lawrence; Moomaw, William and Gallagher, Kevin (eds) *Transboundary Environmental Negotiation: New Approaches to Global Cooperation* (Jossey-Bass, San Francisco, 2002) 3.

Noyes, John E "The Common Heritage of Mankind: Past, Present, and Future" (2011) 40(1-3) Denver Journal of International Law and Policy 447.

Ondřej, Jan "From the Common Heritage of Mankind to Commercialization and Back Again?" in International Institute of Space Law of the International Astronautical Federation *Proceedings of the Forty-Third Colloquium on the Law of Outer Space: October 2–6, 2000, Rio de Janeiro, Brazil* (American Institute of Aeronautics and Astronautics, Reston, 2001) 18.

Orrego-Vicuña, Francisco "El patrimonio común de la humanidad" in *Los fondos marinos y oceanicos* (Editorial Andres Bello, Santiago, 1976) 219.

Paolillo, Felipe H "Naturaleza jurídica del principio del 'patrimonio común de la humanidad'" (paper prepared for the 13th Congress of the Instituto Hispano-Luso-Americano de Derecho Internacional, Lima, 8–13 November 1982).
— "Naturaleza jurídica del principio del 'patrimonio común de la humanidad'" (1984) 7 Anuario Hispano-Luso-Americano de Derecho Internacional 353.

Paquerot, Sylvie "Les exigences de l'état de droit dans le concept de patrimoine commun de l'humanité: réflexion autour de la mise en représentation de la légitimité au plan international" in Mockle, Daniel and others *Mondialisation et état de droit* (Bruylant, Brussels, 2002) 321.
— *Le statut des ressources vitales en droit international: essai sur le concept de patrimoine commun de l'humanité* (Bruylant, Brussels, 2002).

Pardo, Arvid "The Common Heritage of Mankind" (1983) 2 Development 6.
— and Christol, Carl Q "The Common Interest: Tension Between the Whole and the Parts" in Macdonald, Ronald StJ and Johnston, Douglas M (eds) *The Structure and Process of International Law: Essays in Legal Philosophy, Doctrine and Theory* (Martinus Nijhoff Publishers, The Hague, 1983) 643.

Pasquali, Leonardo "Patrimonio comune dell'umanità e limiti allo sfruttamento di certe risorse" (2007) 4 Rivista di Diritto Agrario [Istituto di Diritto Agrario Internazionale e Comparato, Milan] 719.

Payoyo, Peter B "The Common Heritage of Mankind and Global Environmental Governance" (paper presented to the 4th Conference of the International Association for the Study of Common Property, Manila, 16–19 June 1993).

Perrakis, Stelios E *To dikaiōma stēn apolaysē tēs koinēs klēronomias tēs anorōpotētas ōs dikaiōma allēeggyēs (mia prōte prodeggidē)* = *Le droit de bénéficier du patrimoine commun de l'humanité comme droit de solidarité (une premiére approche)* (Editions AN Sakkoulas, Athens, 1982). Greek.

Pinto, Moragodage CW "'Common Heritage of Mankind': From Metaphor to Myth, and the Consequences of Constructive Ambiguity" in Makarczyk, Jerzy (ed) *Theory of International Law at the Threshold of the 21st Century: Essays in Honour of Krzysztof Skubiszewski* (Kluwer Law International, The Hague, 1996) 249.
— "The Common Heritage of Mankind: Then and Now" (2012) 361 Recueil des Cours de l'Académie de Droit International de la Haye = Collected Courses of the Hague Academy of International Law 9.

Pop, Virgiliu "The Common Heritage of Mankind: Reaping Without Sowing" in *Who Owns the Moon? Extraterrestrial Aspects of Land and Mineral Resources Ownership* (Springer, Dordrecht, 2008) 121.

Porritt, Jonathon "The Common Heritage: What Heritage? Common to Whom?" (1992) 1(3) Environmental Values 257.
— "The Common Heritage: What Heritage? Common to Whom?" (Global Security Lecture to the University of Cambridge, Cambridge, 23 January 1992).

Postyšhev, Vladimir M "The Concept of the 'Common Heritage of Mankind' in Politics and International Law" (1989) 20(4) Korean Journal of International Studies 627.
— "The Concept of the Common Heritage of Mankind in Politics and International Law" (paper presented to the 17th Annual Conference of Pacem in Maribus, Moscow, 26–30 June 1989).
— *The Concept of the Common Heritage of Mankind: From New Thinking to New Practice* (Gayane Chalyan trans, Progress Publishers, Moscow, 1990).

— and Danilenko, Gennady M "Koncepciâ obŝego naslediâ čelovečestva i meždunarodnogo prava: dva podhoda k probleme" [The Conception of Common Heritage of Mankind and International Law: Two Approaches to a Problem] (1988) 6 Sovetskoe Gosudarstvo i Pravo [Soviet State and Law] 89. Russian.

Przyborowska-Klimczak, Anna "Human Rights and the Concept of the Common Heritage of Mankind" in Leszczynski, Leszek (ed) *Protection of Human Rights in Poland and the European Communities* (2nd ed, Den Bosch (NL), BookWorld Publications, 1997) 71.

Pureza, José M "Globalização e direito internacional: da boa vizinhança ao patrimônio comum da humanidade" (1993) 36 Revista Crítica de Ciências Sociais [Centro de Estudos Sociais, Coimbra] 9.
— "Egalité juridique, inégalité économique et patrimoine commun de l'humanité. Le probléme institutionnel" in Université de Poitiers, Faculté de Droit et Sciences Sociales *Mélanges offerts à Jorge Campinos* (Presses Universitaires de France, Paris, 1996) 381.
— *O património comum da humanidade: rumo a um direito internacional da solidariedade?* (Edições Afrontamento, Porto (PT), 1998).
— *El patrimonio común de la humanidad, ¿hacia un derecho internacional de la solidaridad?* (Editorial Trotta, Madrid, 2002).
— "Defensive and Oppositional Counter-Hegemonic Uses of International Law: From the International Criminal Court to the Common Heritage of Humankind" in de Sousa Santos, Boaventura and Rodríguez-Garavito, César A (eds) *Law and Globalization from Below: Towards a Cosmopolitan Legality* (Cambridge University Press, Cambridge, 2005) 267.

Rajagopalan, R (ed) *Common Heritage and the 21st Century: Proceedings of Pacem in Maribus XXV: November 1997* (International Ocean Institute in cooperation with the

Foundation for International Studies and Government of Malta, Mside (MT), 1998).
— "Common Heritage: The Eco-Village Approach" in *Common Heritage and the 21st Century: Proceedings of Pacem in Maribus XXV: November 1997* (International Ocean Institute in cooperation with Foundation for International Studies and Government of Malta, Mside (MT), 1998) 159.

Ramos, CT "Governance: Politics as Grounds for 'Common Heritage of Humanity'" in Amoêda, Rogério; Lira, Sérgio and Pinheiro, Cristina (eds) *Heritage 2010: Heritage and Sustainable Development: Proceedings of the 2nd International Conference on Heritage and Sustainable Development, Evora, Portugal, 22–26 June* (Green Lines Institute for Sustainable Development, Barcelos (PT), 2010) 219.

Rangnekar, Dwijen "Common Heritage or Private Property?" (1996) 26(6) Ecologist 268.

Reisman, Michael [Introduction to the Panel] "'The Common Heritage of Mankind': Success or Failure of International Regulation?" in Canadian Council on International Law = Conseil Canadien de Droit International (ed) *International Regulation and Deregulation: Emerging Trends in the Role of International Institutions: Proceedings: XIV Annual Conference: October 17–19, 1985, Ottawa, Ontario = Réglementation et déréglementation internationale: évolution du rôle des institutions internationales: travaux: 17–19 octobre 1985, Ottawa, Ontario* (Canadian Council on International Law, Ottawa, 1986) 228.

Rigaux, François "Le droit de propriété sur le patrimoine commun de l'humanité" (lecture manuscript held at Institut International des Droits de l'Homme, Strasbourg, 1979).

Riphagen, Willem "The International Concern for the Environment as Expressed in the Concepts of the 'Common

Heritage of Mankind' and of 'Shared Natural Resources'" in Bothe, Michael (ed) *Trends in Environmental Policy and Law = Tendances actuelles de la politique et du droit de l'environnement* (International Union for Conservation of Nature and Natural Resources, Gland (CH), 1980) 343.

Romi, Raphaël "Sur la notion de patrimoine commun de l'humanité en droit de l'environnement" (1989) 67–68 Actes 64.
— "L'environnement, comme patrimoine commun de l'humanité: la fonction environnementale du droit de propriété" in Argullol i Murgadas, Enric (ed) *La dimensión ambiental del territorio frente a los derechos patrimoniales: un reto para la protección efectiva del medio natural* (Tirant Lo Blanch, Valencia, 2004) 19.

Ross, David A "What Common Heritage!" (1973) 17 Oceanus 2.

Saigal, Krishan "Security, Co-Development of Technology and the Common Heritage of Mankind" (paper presented to the 17th Annual Conference of Pacem in Maribus, Moscow, 26–30 June 1989).

Schembri, Guzeppi *The Common Heritage of Mankind: Towards Definition and Initiative* (Publishers Enterprises Group, Marsa (MT), 1988).
— *The Common Heritage of Mankind: Quantum Theory of Human Relations* (Publishers Enterprises Group, Marsa (MT), 1990).

Scholtz, Werner "Common Heritage: Saving the Environment for Humankind or Exploiting Resources in the Name of Eco-Imperialism?" (2008) 41(2) Comparative and International Law Journal of Southern Africa 273.

Schrijver, Nico "Permanent Sovereignty over Natural Resources versus the Common Heritage of Mankind: Complementary or Contradictory Principles of International Economic Law?" in de Waart, Paul; Peters, Paul and

Denters, Erik (eds) *International Law and Development* (Martinus Nijhoff Publishers, Dordrecht, 1988) 87.
— "De teloorgang van het gemeenschappelijk erfgoed der mensheid" [The Withering Away of the Common Heritage of Mankind] (1999) 48 Ars Aequi 405. Dutch.
— "Permanent Sovereignty over Natural Resources versus the Common Heritage of Mankind: Complementary or Contradictory Principles of International Economic Law?" in Hunter, David; Salzman, James and Zaelke, Durwood *International Environmental Law and Policy* (3rd ed, Foundation Press, New York, 2007) 486.

Serracino Inglott, Peter "The Common Heritage of Mankind – A Roman Catholic View" (paper presented to the 17th Annual Conference of Pacem in Maribus, Moscow, 26–30 June 1989).
— "The Common Heritage and the Rights of Future Generations" in Busuttil, Salvino and others (eds) *Our Responsibilities Towards Future Generations: A Programme of UNESCO and the International Environment Institute* (Foundation for International Studies, University of Malta, Valletta, 1990) 67.
— "The Common Heritage and Future Generations" in Agius, Emmanuel and Busuttil, Salvino (eds) *What Future for Future Generations? A Programme of UNESCO and the International Environment Institute* (Foundation for International Studies, University of Malta, Valletta, 1994) 195.
— "De-Platonising the Guardian in the Context of the Rights of Future Generations" in Busuttil, Salvino and Busuttil, David R (eds) *Telos Vol IV: What Future for Future Generations?* (Fondation de Malte, Valletta, 2010) 9.
— "Correlatives of the Common Heritage and the Present Euro-Mediterranean Context" in Attard, David J and Martínez Gutiérrez, Norman A (eds) *Serving the Rule of International Maritime Law: Essays in Honour of Professor David Joseph Attard* (Routledge, London, 2010) 176.

Shackelford, Scott J "The Tragedy of the Common Heritage of Mankind" (2009) 28(1) Stanford Environmental Law Journal 109.

Shraga, Daphna "The Common Heritage of Mankind: The Concept and its Application" (1986) 15 Annales d'Études Internationales = Annals of International Studies 45.

Slatinek, Stanislav "Legal-Ethical Reflection on Globalisation, Common Heritage of Nations" in Juhant, Janez and Žalec, Bojan (eds) *Surviving Globalization: The Uneasy Gift of Interdependence = Überleben mit der globalisierung: das schwierige geschenk der interdependenz* (Lit Verlag, Berlin, 2008) 191.

Smouts, Marie-Claude "Du patrimoine commun de l'humanité aux biens publics globaux" in Cormier-Salem, Marie-Christine and others (eds) *Patrimoines naturels au sud: territoires, identités et stratégies locales* (Institut de Recherche pour le Développement (IRD) Éditions, Montpellier, 2005) 53.

Song, Yong S "Common Heritage of Mankind as a Customary International Norm: The USA, USSR and ROK" (1984) 8(3) Korea and World Affairs 665.

Sreenivasa Rao, Pemmaraju "Environment as a Common Heritage of Mankind: A Policy Perspective" in Pellet, Alain (ed) *International Law on the Eve of the Twenty-First Century: Views from the International Law Commission = Le droit international à l'aube du XXIe siècle: réflexions de codificateurs* (United Nations, New York, 1997) 201.

Stańczyk, Janusz "Pojęcie wspólnego dziedzictwa ludzkości w prawie międzynarodowym" [The Notion of Common Heritage of Mankind in International Law] (1985) 40(9) Państwo i Prawo [State and Law] 55. Polish.

Stec, Stephen "Humanitarian Limits to Sovereignty: Common Concern and Common Heritage Approaches to

Natural Resources and Environment" (2010) 12(3) International Community Law Review 361.

Stenson, Anthony J and Gray, Tim S "Common Heritage of Mankind" in *The Politics of Genetic Resource Control* (Macmillan Press, Houndmills (UK), 1999) 136.

Stocker, Werner *Das prinzip des common heritage of mankind als ausdruck des staatengemeinschaftsinteresses im völkerrecht* (Schulthess Juristische Medien, Zürich, 1993).

Sucharitkul, Sompong "Évolution continue d'une notion nouvelle: le patrimoine commun de l'humanité" in Food and Agriculture Organization of the United Nations (ed) *Essays in Memory of Jean Carroz: The Law and the Sea = Mélanges à la mémoire de Jean Carroz: le droit et la mer = Ensayos en memoria de Jean Carroz: el derecho y el mar* (FAO, Rome, 1987) 267.
— "Évolution continue d'une notion nouvelle: le patrimoine commun de l'humanité" in Dinstein, Yoram and Tabory, Mala (eds) *International Law at a Time of Perplexity – Essays in Honour of Shabtai Rosenne* (Martinus Nijhoff Publishers, Dordrecht, 1989) 887.
— "Évolution d'une notion nouvelle: le patrimoine commun de l'humanité" (presentation to a Conference of the Centre de Recherche en Droit Public, Université de Montréal, Montréal, 1 November 2006).

Suter, Keith "The Common Heritage of Humankind – Where to Next?" (1986) 14(5) Habitat Australia 8.
— "The Common Heritage of Humankind" in *Antarctica: Private Property or Public Heritage?* (Zed Books, London, 1991) 159.

Tams, Christian J [Addendum] "Common Heritage of Mankind" in Volger, Helmut (ed) *A Concise Encyclopedia of the United Nations* (2nd revised ed, Martinus Nijhoff Publishers, Leiden, 2010) 50.

Tarlock, AD "The Great Lakes as an Environmental Heritage of Humankind: An International Law Perspective" (2007) 40(4) University of Michigan Journal of Law Reform 995.

Tatsuzawa, Kunihiko "Political and Legal Meaning of the Common Heritage of Mankind" in International Institute of Space Law of the International Astronautical Federation *Proceedings of the Twenty-Ninth Colloquium on the Law of Outer Space: October 4–11, 1986, Innsbruck, Austria* (American Institute of Aeronautics and Astronautics, New York, 1987) 84.

Taylor, Prue "The Common Heritage of Mankind" in *An Ecological Approach to International Law: Responding to Challenges of Climate Change* (Routledge, London, 1998) 258.
— "Common Heritage of Mankind Principle" in Bosselmann, Klaus; Fogel, Daniel S and Ruhl, JB (eds) *Berkshire Encyclopedia of Sustainability: Law and Politics of Sustainability* (Berkshire Publishing Group, Great Barrington, 2010) 64.
— "The Common Heritage Principle and Public Health: Honouring Our Legacy" in Westra, Laura; Soskolne, Colin and Spady, Donald (eds) *Human Health and Ecological Integrity: Ethics, Law and Human Rights* (Routledge, London, 2012) 43.
— "Das gemeinsame erbe der menschheit" in Helfrich, Silke and Heinrich-Böll-Stiftung (eds) *Commons: für eine neue politik jenseits von markt und staat* (Transcript Verlag, Bielefeld (DE), 2012) 426.
— "The Common Heritage of Mankind: A Bold Doctrine Kept Within Strict Boundaries" in Bollier, David and Helfrich, Silke (eds) *The Wealth of the Commons: A World Beyond Market and State* (Levellers, Amherst, 2012) 353.
— "The Future of the Common Heritage of Mankind: Intersections with the Public Trust Doctrine" in Westra, Laura; Taylor, Prue E and Michelot, Agnès (eds) *Confronting Ecological and Economic Collapse: Ecological*

Integrity for Law, Policy and Human Rights (Routledge, Abingdon, 2013) 32.

Thomas, Zakir "Common Heritage to Common Concern: Preserving a Heritage and Sharing Knowledge" (2005) 8(3) Journal of World Intellectual Property 241.

Tieya, Wang "The Concept of a Common Heritage of Mankind" (1984) Zhong Guo Guo Ji Fa Nian Kan [Chinese Yearbook of International Law] 19. Chinese.

Travieso, Juan A "El patrimonio común de la humanidad en el nuevo orden internacional" (1981) 41(2) Revista del Colegio de Abogados de Buenos Aires 1.

Treves, Tullio "Judicial Action for the Common Heritage" in Hestermeyer, Holger and others (eds) *Law of the Sea in Dialogue* (Springer, Heidelberg, 2011) 113.

Trindade, Antônio AC "Conceptual Constructions: Common Heritage of Mankind and Common Concern of Mankind" (2005) 316 Recueil des Cours de l'Académie de Droit International de la Haye = Collected Courses of the Hague Academy of International Law 365.
— "Conceptual Constructions: Common Heritage of Mankind and Common Concern of Mankind" in *International Law for Humankind: Towards a New Jus Gentium* (2nd revised ed, Martinus Nijhoff Publishers, Leiden, 2013) 327.

Tronchetti, Fabio "The Common Heritage of Mankind" in *The Exploitation of Natural Resources of the Moon and Other Celestial Bodies: A Proposal for a Legal Regime* (Martinus Nijhoff Publishers, Leiden, 2009) 85.

Tuerk, Helmut "The Idea of the Common Heritage of Mankind" in Attard, David J and Martínez Gutiérrez, Norman A (eds) *Serving the Rule of International Maritime Law: Essays in Honour of Professor David Joseph Attard* (Routledge, London, 2010) 157.

— "The Principle of the Common Heritage of Mankind" in *Reflections on the Contemporary Law of the Sea* (Martinus Nijhoff Publishers, Leiden, 2012) 31.

van Ettinger, Jan; King, Alexander and Payoyo, Peter "The Common Heritage of Mankind and Four Other Problem Areas" in Payoyo, Peter (ed) *Ocean Governance: Sustainable Development of the Seas* (United Nations University Press, Tokyo, 1994) 248.

van Hoof, Godefridus JH "Legal Status of the Concept of the Common Heritage of Mankind" (1986) 7 Grotiana 49.

van Hoorick, Geert "The Principle of Common Heritage of Mankind as Basis for a World Ecological Constitution" in Tunytsya, Yuriy (ed) *Ekologìčna konstitucìâ zemlì. Ìdeâ. Koncepcìâ. Problemi* [World Ecological Constitution: Idea, Concept, Problems] (Publishing Centre of Ivan Franko National University of Lviv, Lviv (UA), 2002) 156.

Vukas, Budislav "Zajednička baština čovječanstva" [Common Heritage of Mankind] (1981–82) Godišnjak Institut za Međunarodno Politiku i Privredu (Belgrade) [Yearbook of the Institute of International Politics and Economics] 190. Serbo-Croatian.
— "The Common Heritage of Mankind: A Legal Concept for the Survival of Humanity" in Bulajić, Milan; Pindić, Dimitrije and Marinković, Momirka (eds) *The Charter of Economic Rights and Duties of States: Ten Years of Implementation. The Proceedings of the First Yugoslav International Seminar on Legal Aspects of the New International Economic Order: Beograd, April 11–13, 1985* (Institute of International Politics and Economics/The Macroproject of Institute Consortium on New International Economic Order, Belgrade, 1986) 209.
— "Common Heritage of Mankind: A Legal Concept for the Survival of Humanity" in *Law of the Sea: Selected Writings* (Martinus Nijhoff Publishers, Leiden, 2004) 125.

White, Mary V "The Common Heritage of Mankind: An Assessment" (1982) 14(3) Case Western Reserve Journal of International Law 509.

Wolfrum, Rüdiger "The Principle of the Common Heritage of Mankind" (1983) 43(2) Zeitschrift für Ausländisches Öffentliches Recht und Völkerrecht 312.
— "Common Heritage of Mankind" in Wolfrum, Rüdiger (ed) *The Max Planck Encyclopedia of Public International Law* (Oxford University Press, online edition <http://www.mpepil.com>).

Wünsche, Harry "The Principle of the Common Heritage of Mankind" in United Nations Institute for Training and Research *Progressive Development of the Principles and Norms of International Law Relating to the New International Economic Order: Analytical Papers and Analysis of Texts of Relevant Documents* (UNITAR, New York, 1983) vol 2, 437.

Yu, Jia "Safeguarding the Common Heritage of Mankind" (paper presented to the briefing for the 15th Session of the International Seabed Authority, Kingston (JM), 2 June 2009).

Zuleta, Bernardo "The Common Heritage" (1977) 11 Marine Technology Society Journal 3.

2. CHM in Multi-Subject Areas

Cunningham, Francis X "The Common Heritage: An Overview of the International Laws That Call for Sharing Global and Celestial Wealth" (1981) 58 Foreign Service Journal 13.

Frakes, Jennifer "The Common Heritage of Mankind Principle and the Deep Seabed, Outer Space, and Antarctica: Will Developed and Developing Nations Reach a Compromise?" (2003) 21(2) Wisconsin International Law Journal 409.

Imber, Mark "International Institutions and the Common Heritage of Mankind: Sea, Space and the Polar Regions" in Taylor, Paul G and Groom, Arthur JR (eds) *International Institutions at Work* (Frances Pinter Publishers, London, 1988) 150.

Nicholson, Graham "The Common Heritage of Mankind and Mining: An Analysis of the Law as to the High Seas, Outer Space, the Antarctic and World Heritage" (2002) 6 New Zealand Journal of Environmental Law 177.

Niciu, Martian I "Le patrimoine commun de l'humanité en droit international maritime et en droit spatial (quelques considérations)" (1995) 13 Annuaire de Droit Maritime et Aéro-Spatial 9.

Vajić, Nina "The Law of Outer Space and the Law of the Sea: A Joint Contribution to the Emergence of the Common Heritage of Mankind Concept" in Vukas, Budislav (ed) *Essays on the New Law of the Sea* (Institut za Međunarodno Pravo i Međunarodne Odnose, Sveučilišta u Zagrebu [Institute of International and Comparative Law, University of Zagreb], Zagreb, 1985) 537.

3. CHM in the Outer Space Context

Akbar, Sabine *La lune patrimoine commun de l'humanité? Comment exploiter les ressources lunaires dans le respect du droit international* (Institut Français des Relations Internationales, Paris, 2006).

Arzinger, Rainer "On the Legal Contents and Significance of the CHM in Outer Space Law" in International Institute of Space Law of the International Astronautical Federation *Proceedings of the Twenty-Eighth Colloquium on the Law of Outer Space: October 7–12, 1985, Stockholm, Sweden* (American Institute of Aeronautics and Astronautics, New York, 1985) 208.

Back Impallomeni, Elisabeth "Sfruttamento delle risorse della luna e patrimonio comune dell'umanità" in Catalano Sgrosso, Gabriella (ed) *Diritto dello spazio – recenti sviluppi e prospettive = Outer Space Law – New Developments and Prospects. Atti del convegno internazionale organizzato dall'istituto di diritto internazionale della facoltà di economia e commercio della l Università di Roma 'la sapienza': Roma 13–14 marzo 1992* (CEDAM, Padova, 1994) 225.

Bhat, Sandeep B "The Concept of Common Heritage of Mankind in the Governance of the Moon – An Insight into Article 11 of the Moon Agreement" (2007) 1 Legal Opus 92.

Blaser, Arthur W "The Common Heritage in its Infinite Variety: Space Law and the Moon in the 1990s" (1990) 5(1) Journal of Law and Technology 79.

Budišin-Lukin, Milan "Common Heritage of Mankind and the Law of Outer Space" in Bulajić, Milan; Pindić, Dimitrije and Marinković, Momirka (eds) *The Charter of Economic Rights and Duties of States: Ten Years of Implementation.*

The Proceedings of the First Yugoslav International Seminar on Legal Aspects of the New International Economic Order: Beograd, April 11–13, 1985 (Institute of International Politics and Economics/The Macroproject of Institute Consortium on New International Economic Order, Belgrade, 1986) 221.

Buxton, Carol R "Property in Outer Space: The Common Heritage of Mankind Principle vs. the 'First in Time, First in Right' Rule of Property Law" (2004) 69(4) Journal of Air Law and Commerce 689.

Christol, Carl Q "The Common Heritage of Mankind Provision in the 1979 Agreement Governing the Activities of States on the Moon and Other Celestial Bodies" (1980) 14(3) International Lawyer 429.
— *The Common Heritage of Mankind Provision in the 1979 Agreement Governing the Activities of States on the Moon and Other Celestial Bodies* (report prepared for the Centre for Research of Air and Space Law, McGill University, Montréal, 1980).
— *The Common Heritage of Mankind Provision of the 1979 Agreement Governing the Activities of States on the Moon and Other Celestial Bodies* (University of Southern California, Los Angeles, 1980).
— *The Spectrum and Orbital Position Resources: The Common Heritage of Mankind in the Moon Treaty* (report prepared for the Centre for Research of Air and Space Law, McGill University, Montréal, 1980).
— "The Common Heritage of Mankind Provisions of the 5 December 1979 Moon Treaty" (1982) 6 Annuaire de Droit Maritime et Aérien 429.
— "The Common Heritage of Mankind Provisions of the 5 December 1979 Moon Treaty" in *Space Law: Past, Present and Future* (Kluwer Law and Taxation Publishers, Deventer, 1991) 403.

Cocca, Aldo A "Carácter de la misión de los cosmonautas ante la incorporación de la luna al patrimonio común de la humanidad" (paper presented to the 7th Congress of the

Instituto Hispano-Luso-Americano de Derecho Internacional, Buenos Aires, 12 August 1969).

— "The Principle of the 'Common Heritage of All Mankind' as Applied to Natural Resources from Outer Space and Celestial Bodies" in International Institute of Space Law of the International Astronautical Federation *Proceedings of the Sixteenth Colloquium on the Law of Outer Space: October 17–13, 1973, Baku, USSR* (University of California School of Law, Davis, 1974) 172.

— "The Radio Spectrum Resource as a Common Heritage of Mankind" (lecture to the University of Hawaii, Honolulu, 16 September 1976).

— "The Common Heritage of Mankind: Doctrine and Principle of Space Law – An Overview" in International Institute of Space Law of the International Astronautical Federation *Proceedings of the Twenty-Ninth Colloquium on the Law of Outer Space: October 4–11, 1986, Innsbruck, Austria* (American Institute of Aeronautics and Astronautics, New York, 1987) 17.

— "Revaluation of the Concept of the Human Condition and the Common Heritage of Mankind: Keys to the Social Benefits of Space Technology" (1989) 19(9) Acta Astronautica 779.

— "Protocol to the Space Treaty on the Common Heritage of Mankind Principle" in International Institute of Space Law of the International Astronautical Federation *Proceedings of the Thirty-Fourth Colloquium on the Law of Outer Space: October 5–12, 1991, Montréal, Canada* (American Institute of Aeronautics and Astronautics, Reston, 1992) 161.

de Faramiñán Gilbert, Juan M "The Common Heritage of Mankind Principle: The Moon and Lunar Resources" in International Institute of Space Law of the International Astronautical Federation *Proceedings of the Fifty-Second Colloquium on the Law of Outer Space: October 12–16, 2009, Daejeon, Republic of Korea* (American Institute of Aeronautics and Astronautics, Reston, 2010) 504.

Dekanozov, Reginald V "The 'Common Heritage of Mankind' in the 1979 Agreement Governing the Activities of States on the Moon and Other Celestial Bodies" in International Institute of Space Law of the International Astronautical Federation *Proceedings of the Twenty-Fourth Colloquium on the Law of Outer Space: September 6–12, 1981, Rome, Italy* (American Institute of Aeronautics and Astronautics, New York, 1982) 181.

— "Outer Space, Celestial Bodies and their Resources. 'The Common Heritage of Mankind'" in Fedoseev, Petr N and others *Space and Law = Kosmos i pravo* ('Social Sciences Today' Editorial Board, USSR Academy of Sciences, Moscow, 1985) 8.

Ervin, Scott "Law in a Vacuum: The Common Heritage Doctrine in Outer Space Law" (1984) 7(2) Boston College International and Comparative Law Review 403.

Fountain, Lynn M "Creating Momentum in Space: Ending the Paralysis Produced by the 'Common Heritage of Mankind' Doctrine" (2003) 35(4) Connecticut Law Review 1753.

Gabrynowicz, Joanne I "The 'Province' and 'Heritage' of Mankind Reconsidered: A New Beginning" in Mendell, Wendell W (ed) *The Second Conference on Lunar Bases and Space Activities of the 21st Century: Papers from a Conference Sponsored by Lyndon B. Johnson Space Center and the Lunar and Planetary Institute, and Held in Houston, Texas, April 5–7, 1988* (National Aeronautics and Space Administration, Washington (DC), 1992) 691.

Gangale, Thomas "Common Heritage in Magnificent Desolation: The Moon Agreements' Tragic Odyssey" in *The Development of Outer Space: Sovereignty and Property Rights in International Space Law* (Praeger, Westport (US), 2009) 67.

Górbiel, Andrzej "'Common Heritage of Mankind' Concept in the Space Law – Doctrine and Codification Works of the

United Nations" (1981) 20 Il Diritto Aereo: Rivista Trimestrale di Dottrina, Giurisprudenza e Legislazione 59.
— "International Regulation of the Use of the Lunar Resources and the Common Heritage of Mankind Doctrine" (1983) 9 Acta Universitatis Lodziensis: Politologia [Uniwersytet Łódzki, Łódź] 12.

Gorove, Stephen [report, Session on] "'Outer Space, International Law, International Regimes and the Common Heritage of Mankind', Association of the Bar of the City of New York, New York, N.Y., November 14, 1981" (1982) 10(1) Journal of Space Law 65.
— "Resources of the Moon and Other Celestial Bodies as Mankind's Common Heritage" (1983) 181 Recueil des Cours de l'Académie de Droit International de la Haye = Collected Courses of the Hague Academy of International Law 370.
— "Utilization of the Natural Resources of the Space Environment in the Light of the Concept of Common Heritage of Mankind" in Dupuy, René-Jean (ed) *Le règlement des différends sur les nouvelles ressources naturelles = The Settlement of Disputes on the New Natural Resources* (Workshop of the Hague Academy of International Law and United Nations University, The Hague, 8–10 November 1982; Martinus Nijhoff Publishers, The Hague, 1983) 105.
— "Utilization of the Natural Resources of the Space Environment in the Light of the Concept of Common Heritage of Mankind" in Snyder, Frederick E and Sathirathai, Surakiart (eds) *Third World Attitudes Toward International Law: An Introduction* (Martinus Nijhoff Publishers, Dordrecht, 1987) 775.

Hobe, Stephan "Common Heritage of Mankind – An Outdated Concept in International Space Law?" in International Institute of Space Law of the International Astronautical Federation *Proceedings of the Forty-First Colloquium on the Law of Outer Space: 28 September – 2 October, 1998, Melbourne, Australia* (American Institute of Aeronautics and Astronautics, Reston, 1999) 271.

— "ILA Resolution 1/2002 with Regard to the Common Heritage of Mankind Principle in the Moon Agreement" in International Institute of Space Law of the International Astronautical Federation *Proceedings of the Forty-Seventh Colloquium on the Law of Outer Space: October 4–8, 2004, Vancouver, Canada* (American Institute of Aeronautics and Astronautics, Reston, 2005) 536.

— "ILA Resolution 1/2002 with Regard to the Common Heritage of Mankind Principle in the Moon Agreement" in Kerrest, Armel (ed) *L'adaption du droit de l'espace à ses nouveaux défis: liber amicorum: mélanges en l'honneur de Simone Courteix* (Éditions A. Pedone, Paris, 2007) 301.

Hoffstadt, Brian M "Moving the Heavens: Lunar Mining and the 'Common Heritage of Mankind' in the Moon Treaty" (1994) 42(2) UCLA Law Review 575.

Irigoin Barrenne, Jeannette "El espacio: ¿patrimonio común de la humanidad?" (1986) 19(75) Estudios Internacionales: Revista del Instituto de Estudios Internacionales de la Universidad de Chile 392.

Jacobs, Benjamin "The Future of Energy: Lunar Resource Management and the Common Heritage of Mankind" (2011-2012) 24 Georgetown International Environmental Law Review 221.

Jasentuliyana, Nandasiri "The UN Space Treaties and the Common Heritage Principle" (1986) 2(4) Space Policy 296.

Kerrest, Armel "Outer Space: Res Communis, Common Heritage or Common Province of Mankind?" (lecture manuscript for the 10th European Centre for Space Law Summer Course on Space Law and Policy, Nice, 27 August – 8 September 2001).

Klimenko, Boris M "The Concept of a Common Heritage of Mankind in International Outer Space Law" (1986) Diplomatic Herald 184.

Kopal, Vladimir "Progressive Development of Space Law and Concept of Common Heritage of Mankind" in Pałyga, Edward J (ed) *International Space Law Miscellanea: liber amicorum Honouring Professor Dr. Andrzej Górbiel on his 65th Anniversary = Międzynarodowe prawo kosmiczne miscellanea: księga pamiątkowa ofiarowana Prof. Dr. hab. Andrzejowi Górbielowi w 65-lecie urodzin* (Agencja Wydawnicza Fundacji im, Andrzej Frycza Modrzewskiego, Warsaw, 1995) 107.

Lee, Ricky J "Balancing the Competing Interests to Resolve the Impasse over the Effects of the Common Heritage of Mankind Provision in the Moon Agreement" in International Institute of Space Law of the International Astronautical Federation *Proceedings of the Fifty-Third Colloquium on the Law of Outer Space: 27 September – 1 October 2010, Prague, Czech Republic* (American Institute of Aeronautics and Astronautics, Reston, 2011) IAC-10.E7.2.6.
— "Exploitation Rights: Evolving from the 'Province of Mankind' to the 'Common Heritage of Mankind'" in *Law and Regulation of Commercial Mining of Minerals in Outer Space* (Springer, Dordrecht, 2012) 203.

Léger, Brigitte "La lune: patrimoine commun de l'humanité" (1979) 17 Canadian Yearbook of International Law = Annuaire Canadien de Droit International 280.

Maiorsky, Boris "A Few Reflections on the Meaning and the Interrelation of 'Province of All Mankind' and 'Common Heritage of Mankind' Notions" in International Institute of Space Law of the International Astronautical Federation *Proceedings of the Twenty-Ninth Colloquium on the Law of Outer Space: October 4–11, 1986, Innsbruck, Austria* (American Institute of Aeronautics and Astronautics, New York, 1987) 58.

Mani, Venkateshwara S "The Common Heritage of Mankind: Implications for the Legal Status of Property Rights on the Moon and Other Celestial Bodies" in

International Institute of Space Law of the International Astronautical Federation *Proceedings of the Thirty-Ninth Colloquium on the Law of Outer Space: October 7–11, 1996, Beijing, China* (American Institute of Aeronautics and Astronautics, Reston, 1997) 31.

Marín, Cipriano "Starlight: A Common Heritage" in Valls-Gabaud, David and Boksenberg, Alexander (eds) *The Role of Astronomy in Society and Culture: Proceedings of the International Astronomical Union, IAU Symposium 260, 19–23 January 2009, Paris, France* (Cambridge University Press, Cambridge, 2011) 449.

Mateesco-Matte, Nicolas "The Common Heritage of Mankind and Outer Space: Toward a New International Order for Survival" (1987) 12 Annals of Air and Space Law = Annales de Droit Aérien et Spatial 313.

Nandakumar, Sethu "'Common Heritage of Mankind' – Property Rights in the Wake of Commercial Use of the Moon and Other Celestial Bodies" in International Institute of Space Law of the International Astronautical Federation *Proceedings of the Forty-Eighth Colloquium on the Law of Outer Space: October 17–21, 2005, Fukuoka, Japan* (American Institute of Aeronautics and Astronautics, Reston, 2006) 308.

Narayana Rao, K "Common Heritage of Mankind and the Moon Treaty" (1982) 21(2) Indian Journal of International Law 275.

Oduntan, Gbenga "Legality of the Common Heritage of Mankind Principle in Space Law: Reconciliation of the Views from the North and South" (paper presented to the Space Law Symposium of the International Institute of Space Law, Sydney, 6 May 2003).
— "Imagine There Are No Possessions: Legal and Moral Basis of the Common Heritage Principle in Space Law" (2005) 2(1) Manchester Journal of International Economic Law 30.

— "Legality of the Common Heritage of Mankind Principle in Space Law" in *Sovereignty and Jurisdiction in the Airspace and Outer Space: Legal Criteria for Spatial Delimitation* (Routledge, Abingdon (UK), 2011) 191.

— "Imagine There Are No Possessions: Legal and Moral Basis of the Common Heritage Principle in Space Law" in De Feyter, Koen (ed) *Globalization and Common Responsibilities of States* (Ashgate, Farnham (UK), 2013) 259.

Okolie, Charles C "Legal Interpretation of the 1979 United Nations Treaty Concerning the Activities of Sovereign States on the Moon and Other Celestial Bodies Within the Meaning of the Concept of Common Heritage of Mankind" in International Institute of Space Law of the International Astronautical Federation *Proceedings of the Twenty-Third Colloquium on the Law of Outer Space: September 21–28, 1980, Tokyo, Japan* (American Institute of Aeronautics and Astronautics, New York, 1981) 61.

Ospina, Sylvia "Outer Space: 'Common Heritage' or 'Common Junkyard' of Mankind?" in International Institute of Space Law of the International Astronautical Federation *Proceedings of the Thirtieth Colloquium on the Law of Outer Space: October 10–17, 1987, Brighton, United Kingdom* (American Institute of Aeronautics and Astronautics, Reston, 1988) 228.

Porras, Daniel A "The 'Common Heritage' of Outer Space: Equal Benefits for Most of Mankind" (2006) 37(1) California Western International Law Journal 143.

Postyšhev, Vladimir M "Koncepciâ obŝego nslediâ čelovečestva primenitel'no k lune i ee prirodnym resursam" [The Conception of Common Heritage of Mankind as Applied to the Moon and its Natural Resources] (1987) Sovetskij Ežegodnik Meždunarodnogo Prava [Soviet Yearbook of International Law] 223. Russian.

— "WARC-ORB-85 and the Common Heritage of Mankind Concept in Space Law" in International Institute of Space

Law of the International Astronautical Federation *Proceedings of the Twenty-Ninth Colloquium on the Law of Outer Space: October 4–11, 1986, Innsbruck, Austria* (American Institute of Aeronautics and Astronautics, New York, 1987) 134.

Raghav, John A "Outer Space: A Part of the Common Heritage of Humankind" (2008) 3 Madras Law Journal 11.

Rana, Harminderpal S "'The Common Heritage of Mankind' & the Final Frontier: A Revaluation of Values Constituting the International Legal Regime for Outer Space Activities" (paper presented to the 5th Annual Symposium on the Law and Outer Space, Georgetown University Law Center, Washington (DC), 10 October 1993).
— "'The Common Heritage of Mankind' & the Final Frontier: A Revaluation of Values Constituting the International Legal Regime for Outer Space Activities" (1994) 26(1) Rutgers Law Journal 225.

Rao, Rega J "Outer Space: A Part of Common Heritage of Mankind" in Mani, Venkateshwara S; Bhatt, Saligram and Balakista Reddy, Vundhyala (eds) *Recent Trends in International Space Law and Policy* (Lancers Books, New Delhi, 1997) 191.

Rosenfield, Stanely B "Solar Energy and the 'Common Heritage of Mankind'" in International Institute of Space Law of the International Astronautical Federation *Proceedings of the Twenty-First Colloquium on the Law of Outer Space: October 3–5, 1978, Dubrovnik, Yugoslavia* (University of California School of Law, Davis, 1979) 58.

Rothblatt, Martin A "International Cooperation in Regulating 12 GHz Band Geostationary Satellite Communications: Technology, Geopolitics and the Common Heritage of Mankind" in International Institute of Space Law of the International Astronautical Federation *Proceedings of the Twenty-Third Colloquium on the Law of Outer Space: September 21–28, 1980, Tokyo, Japan*

(American Institute of Aeronautics and Astronautics, New York, 1981) 189.

Sehgal, Neeru "The Concept of Common Heritage of Mankind under the Moon Treaty, 1979" (1986) 26(1–2) Indian Journal of International Law 106.

Smith, Delbert D "Space Stations and the Common Heritage of Mankind" in *Space Stations – International Law and Policy* (Westview Press, Boulder (US), 1979) 150.

Stańczyk, Janusz "Pojecie wspólnego dziedzictwa ludzkości w prawie kosmicznym" [The Notion of the Common Heritage of Mankind in Outer Space Law] (1987) 3–4 Studia Prawnicze [Legal Studies] 213. Polish.

Talaie, Farhad "The Radio Frequency Spectrum and the Geostationary Satellite Orbit: Common Heritage of Mankind" in Lavery, William J (ed) *Proceedings of the International Conference on Telecommunications: Bridging East & West Through Communications* (Monash University, Clayton (AU), 1997) 1145.

Wijkman, Per M and Wilborg, Clas G "Global Use and Regulation of Space Activities under the Common Heritage Principle" in McGill University, Institute of Air and Space Law *Space Activities and Implications: Where From and Where To at the Threshold of the 80's: Proceedings of the Symposium Held on October 16–17, 1980 = Les activités spatiales et leurs implications, d'où vient-on et où va-t-on à l'aube des années 80: rapports du symposium tenu les 16 et 17 octobre 1980* (Institute and Centre of Air and Space Law, McGill University, Montréal, 1981) 119.

Williams, Sylvia M "The Common Heritage of Mankind and the Moon Agreement: Economic Implications and Institutional Arrangements" in International Institute of Space Law of the International Astronautical Federation *Proceedings of the Twenty-Fourth Colloquium on the Law of Outer Space: September 6–12, 1981, Rome, Italy*

(American Institute of Aeronautics and Astronautics, New York, 1982) 87.

Wolter, Detlev "The Peaceful Purpose Standard of the Common Heritage of Mankind Principle in Outer Space Law" (1985) 9 ASILS International Law Journal 117.
— *Grundlagen 'gemeinsamer sicherheit' im weltraum nach universellem völkerrecht: der grundsatz der friedlichen nutzung des weltraums im lichte des völkerrechtlichen strukturprinzips vom 'gemeinsamen erbe der menschheit'* (Duncker and Humblot, Berlin, 2003).
— "CHOM as a Structural Principle of Outer Space Law" in *Common Security in Outer Space and International Law* (United Nations Institute for Disarmament Research, Geneva, 2006) 99.

Zieck, Marjoleine YA "The Concept of 'Generations' of Human Rights and the Right to Benefit from the Common Heritage of Mankind with Reference to Extraterrestrial Realms" (1992) 25 Verfassung und Recht in Übersee: Law and Politics in Africa, Asia and Latin America 161.

4. CHM in the Marine Context

Adede, Andronico O "The System for Exploitation of the 'Common Heritage of Mankind' at the Caracas Conference" [United Nations Conference on the Law of the Sea] (1975) 69(1) American Journal of International Law 31.

Anand, Ram Prakash "Sea-Bed Beyond National Jurisdiction: A Common Heritage of Mankind" in *Legal Regime of the Sea-Bed and the Developing Countries* (AW Sitjhoff, Leiden, 1976) 177.

Andrassy, Juraj "Pravna narav morskog dna i podzemlja otvorenog mora kao 'baštine čovječanstva'" [The Legal Nature of the Seabed and Subsoil of the High Seas as 'Heritage of Humanity'] (1975) 22(1–2) Jugoslovenska Revija za Međunarodno Pravo [Yugoslav Journal of International Law] 128. Serbo-Croatian.

Arias Stella, Javier "Los fondos marinos, patrimonio común de la humanidad" (1982) 34 Revista Peruana de Derecho Internacional [Sociedad Peruana de Derecho Internacional, Lima] 5.

Artigas de Santamaria, Carmen "The Common Heritage of Mankind: Towards its Rational Administration for the Protection and Preservation of the Marine Environment" in United Nations Environment Programme *Regional Co-operation on Environmental Protection of the Marine and Coastal Areas of the Pacific Basin* (UNEP, Nairobi, 1991) 133.

Baker, Betsy "Uncommon Heritage: Elisabeth Mann Borgese, Pacem in Maribus, the International Ocean Institute and Preparations for UNCLOS III" (2012) 26 Ocean Yearbook 11.

Ballah, Lennox F "The Universality of the 1982 UN Convention on the Law of the Sea: Common Heritage or Common Burden?" in Al-Nauimi, Najeeb and Meese, Richard (eds) *International Legal Issues Arising under the United Nations Decade of International Law* (Martinus Nijhoff Publishers, The Hague, 1995) 339.

Barsegov, Yuri G "Koncepciâ obŝego naslediâ čelovečestva v meždunarodnom morskom prave (teoretičeskie voprosy)" [The Conception of Common Heritage of Mankind in the International Law of the Sea (Theoretical Issues)] (1984) Sovetskij Ežegodnik Meždunarodnogo Prava [Soviet Yearbook of International Law] 47. Russian with summary in English.

Behnam, Awni "Defending Acquired Rights - The Common Heritage Principle and UNCLOS" in Busuttil, Salvino and Busuttil, David R (eds) *Telos Vol V: Special Edition in Honour of Guido de Marco* (Fondation de Malte, Valletta (MT), 2011) 43.

Bencheikh, Madjid "L'intégration de la notion de patrimoine commun de l'humanité dans le système de relations dominant de notre époque: analyse du régime juridique de l'exploitation des fonds des mers (annexe II du texte de négociation composite)" (1978) 15(2) Revue Algérienne des Sciences Juridiques, Èconomiques et Politiques 239.

Bennington, Darise "Law of the Sea: Protecting the Common Heritage of Mankind" (2011) 154 NZLawyer Magazine 24.

Bennouna, Mohamed "Le fond des mers: de 'l'héritage commun et la querelle des héritiers" (1975) 5 Revue Iranienne des Relations Internationales 121.

Beuttler, Theodore M "The Composite Text and Nodule Mining: Over-Regulation as a Threat to the 'Common Heritage of Mankind'" (1977) 1(2) Hastings International and Comparative Law Review 167.

Bhat, Sandeep B "Development of the Concept of Common Heritage of Mankind in Law of the Sea and the 1994 Death-Blow" (2008) 1 Mysore University Law Journal 171.

Biermann, Frank "Tiefseebergbau: vom schicksal eines 'gemeinsamen erbes der menschheit'" (1995) 3–4 Weltwirtschaft & Entwicklung 8.

Boesten, Eke "A Regime for the Ocean Floor Comprising the Common Heritage of Mankind" in *Archaeological and/or Historic Valuable Shipwrecks in International Waters: Public International Law and What It Offers* (TMC Asser Press, The Hague, 2002) 32.

Brodd, Mary J "Common Heritage Approach to Fisheries Through Regional Controls" (1977) 10(1) New York University Journal of International Law and Politics 171.

Brown, Edward D "Freedom of the High Seas versus the Common Heritage of Mankind: Fundamental Principles in Conflict" (1983) 20(3) San Diego Law Review 521.

Carlsson, Annica "The US and UNCLOS III - The Death of the Common Heritage of Humankind Concept?" (1997) 95 Maritime Studies 27.

Caubet, Christian G "La mer comme patrimoine commun de l'humanité: réflexions sur un mythe et une mystification" in Centre d'Études des Relations Internationales (ed) *Discours juridique et pouvoir dans les relations internationales, l'exemple des sujets de droit: actes de la cinquième rencontre de Reims, 28 et 29 juin 1980* (Centre d'Études des Relations Internationales, Faculté de Droit et de Reims, Reims, 1981) 115.

Christy, Francis T "Fisheries: Common Property, Open Access, and the Common Heritage" in Mann Borgese,

Elisabeth (ed) *Pacem in Maribus* (Dodd-Mead, New York, 1972) 183.

Cooke Farrell, Epsey "The Common Heritage of Mankind: Politics of Seabed Mining" in *The Socialist Republic of Vietnam and the Law of the Sea: An Analysis of Vietnamese Behavior Within the Emerging International Oceans Regime* (Martinus Nijhoff Publishers, The Hague, 1998) 132.

Cruickshank, Michael J "Law of the Sea – Common Heritage of Mankind" (2000) 41(2) Sea Technology 117.

Danzig, Aaron L "Sharing the Ocean Treasure: The Common Heritage of All Mankind" (1967) 50 New Leader 11.
— "A Funny Thing Happened to the Common Heritage on the Way to the Sea" (1975) 12(3) San Diego Law Review 655.

Davis, Jerome D and Archer, Clive "Deep Ocean Mining: Who Will Benefit from the 'Common Heritage'?" in Laursen, Finn (ed) *Toward A New International Marine Order* (Martinus Nijhoff Publishers, The Hague, 1982) 151.

Degan, Vladimir-Djuro "The Common Heritage of Mankind in the Present Law of the Sea" in Ando, Nisuke; McWhinney, Edward and Wolfrum, Rüdiger (eds) *Liber amicorum Judge Shigeru Oda* (Kluwer Law International, The Hague, 2002) vol 2, 1363.

Dekanozov, Reginald V "O ponâtii 'obŝee nasledie čelovečestva' v meždunarodnom morskom prave" [On the Notion of 'Common Heritage of Mankind' in the International Law of the Sea] (1982) 9 Sovetskoe Gosudarstvo i Pravo [Soviet State and Law] 89. Russian with summary in English.

Díaz Müller, Luis T "La comisión marítima tripartita del pacífico sur, las 200 millas y el patrimonio común de la humanidad" (1986) 57 Boletín Mexicano de Derecho Comparado 921.

Dragun-Gertner, Maria "Realizacja idei wspólnego dziedzictwa ludzkości ci w działaniach regulacyjnych ISBA" [Implementing the Idea of Common Heritage of Mankind in ISBA Regulatory Actions] in Mika, Cezary and Marciniak, Konrad (eds) *Konwencja NZ o Prawie Morza z 1982 r.: w pietnast rocznicę wejścia w życie* [The UN Convention on the Law of the Sea 1982: The Fifteenth Anniversary of the Entry into Force] (Towarzystwo Naukowe Organizacji i Kierownictwa-Dom Organizatora, Toruń (PL), 2009) 275. Polish.

Dupuy, René-Jean "Le fond des mers: héritage commun de l'humanité" in Dupuy, René-Jean (ed) *Le fond des mers* (Éditions Armand Colin, Paris, 1971) 7.
— "Le fond des mers: héritage commun de l'humanité et le développement" in Société Française pour le Droit International *Colloque d'Aix-en-Provence: pays en voie de développement et transformation du droit international* (Éditions A. Pedone, Paris, 1974) 235.
— "The Notion of Common Heritage of Mankind Applied to the Seabed" in Rozakis, Christos L and Stephanou, Constantine A (eds) *The New Law of the Sea: Selected and Edited Papers of the Athens Colloquium on the Law of the Sea, September 1982* (North-Holland, Elsevier Science Publishers, Amsterdam, 1983) 299.
—"The Notion of the Common Heritage of Mankind Applied to the Seabed" (1983) 8 Annals of Air and Space Law = Annales de Droit Aérien et Spatial 347.
— "La notion de patrimoine commun de l'humanité appliquée aux fonds marins" in Carreau, Dominique and others (eds) *Droit et libertés à la fin du XXe siècle: influence des données économiques et technologiques. Études offertes à Claude-Albert Colliard* (Éditions A. Pedone, Paris, 1984) 197.
— "La zone, patrimoine commun de l'humanité" in Dupuy, René-Jean and Vignes, Daniel (eds) *Traité du nouveau droit de la mer* (Économica, Paris, 1985) 499.
— "The Area as the Common Heritage of Mankind" in Dupuy, René-Jean and Vignes, Daniel (eds) *A Handbook on*

the New Law of the Sea (Martinus Nijhoff Publishers, Dordrecht, 1991) vol 1, 579.
— "La notion de patrimoine commun de l'humanité appliquée aux fonds marins" in Institut du Droit de la Paix et du Développement *Dialectiques du droit international: souveraineté des etats, communauté internationale et droits de l'humanité* (Éditions A. Pedone, Paris, 1999) 189.

Egede, Edwin *Africa and the Deep Seabed Regime: Politics and International Law of the Common Heritage of Mankind* (Springer, Heidelberg, 2011).

Ellingsen Tunold, Betzy M *The UNCLOS III Negotiations on the Deep Sea-Bed Regime: The Common Heritage of Mankind for the Benefit of Mankind as a Whole?* (Fridtjof Nansen Institute, Polhøgda (NO), 1984).

Evensen, Jens "UNCLOS, National Enclosure, and the Common Heritage" in Laursen, Finn (ed) *Toward A New International Marine Order* (Martinus Nijhoff Publishers, The Hague, 1982) 1.

Falk, Richard "Meeting the Challenge of Poverty: Equity, Common Heritage and the Development of Ocean Resources" in Rajagopalan, R (ed) *Common Heritage and the 21st Century: Proceedings of Pacem in Maribus XXV: November 1997* (International Ocean Institute in cooperation with the Foundation for International Studies and Government of Malta, Mside (MT), 1998) 222.

Fletcher, Patrice A *Managing a Common Heritage of Mankind: Issues for the 1973 U.N. Law of the Sea Conference* (Library of Congress, Congressional Research Service, Washington (DC), 1971).

Franckx, Erik "The 200-Mile Limit: Between Creeping Jurisdiction and Creeping Common Heritage?" (2005) 48 German Yearbook of International Law = Jahrbuch für Internationales Recht 117.

— "The 200-Mile Limit: Between Creeping Jurisdiction and Creeping Common Heritage? Some Law of the Sea Considerations from Professor Louis Sohn's Former LL.M. Student" (2007) 39(3) George Washington International Law Review 467.

— "The International Seabed Authority and the Common Heritage of Mankind: The Need for States to Establish the Outer Limits of their Continental Shelf" (2010) 25(4) International Journal of Marine and Coastal Law 543.

Gadkowski, Tadeusz "Koncepcja wspólnego dziedzictwa ludzkości w międzynarodowym prawie morza" [The Concept of the Common Heritage of Mankind in the International Law of the Sea] (1990) 2 Zeszyty Naukowe Instytutu Nauk Społecznych WSI (Koszalin) [Scientific Journal of the Institute of Social Sciences Wyższej Szkoły Inżynierskiej] 269. Polish.

Gelberg, Ludwik "The Freedom of the Seas: Common Heritage of Mankind" in Dupuy, René-Jean (ed) *La gestion des ressources pour l'humanité: le droit de la mer = The Management of Humanity's Resources: The Law of the Sea* (Workshop of the Hague Academy of International Law and United Nations University, The Hague, 29–31 October 1981; Martinus Nijhoff Publishers, The Hague, 1982) 329.

Giarini, Orio "Oceans and the Service Economy: A Note on the Economics of Common Heritage" in The Geneva Association-Association Internationale pour l'Etude de l'Economie de l'Assurance *Études et dossiers no. 252* (The Geneva Association, Geneva, 2002) 105.

Goldwin, Robert A "Le droit de la mer: sens commun contre 'patrimoine commun'" (1985) 89(3) Revue Générale de Droit International Public 719.

Grimming, Jürgen and Schlupp, Christian "Das meer: müllkippe, selbstbedienungsladen oder 'erbe der menschheit'? Anmerkungen zur 3. Seerechtskonferenz der

Vereinten Nationen" (1977) 27(5) Aus Politik und Zeitgeschichte 18.

Guntrip, Edward "The Common Heritage of Mankind: An Adequate Regime for Managing the Deep Seabed?" (2003) 4(2) Melbourne Journal of International Law 376.
— "The Common Heritage of Mankind: An Adequate Regime for Managing the Deep Seabed?" in De Feyter, Koen (ed) *Globalization and Common Responsibilities of States* (Ashgate Publishing, Farnham (UK), 2013) 289.

Gutiérrez Figueroa, Francisco "Principio de patrimonio común de la humanidad en la zona internacional de los fondos marinos" (2010) 7(7) Ius Inter Gentes [Facultad de Derecho de la Pontificia Universidad Católica del Peru] 35.

Halouane, Mohamed Y "Le statut juridique des fonds marins, de l'espace et du plateau continental lors de l'autorité nationale: 'le patrimoine commun de l'humanité'" (1986) 24(2) Revue Algérienne des Sciences Juridiques, Èconomiques et Politiques 410. Arabic.

Harry, Martin A "The Deep Seabed: The Common Heritage of Mankind or Arena for Unilateral Exploitation?" (1992) 40 Naval Law Review 207.

Harvey, Mary K "Oceanic Real Estate: What Constitutes the Common Heritage?" (1972) 9(2) Center Report [Center for the Study of Democratic Institutions, Santa Barbara] 13.

Hayashi, Moritaka "Three Decades' Progress in High Seas Fisheries Governance: Towards a Common Heritage Regime?" in Nordquist, Myron H; Moore, John N and Mahmoudi, Said (eds) *The Stockholm Declaration and Law of the Marine Environment* (Kluwer Law International, The Hague, 2003) 375.

Henley, Peter H "Minerals and Mechanisms: The Legal Significance of the Notion of the 'Common Heritage of Mankind' in the Advisory Opinion of the Seabed Disputes

Chamber" (2011) 12(2) Melbourne Journal of International Law 125.

Hislop, Cheryle "Two Challenges to the Creation of Non-Jurisdictional Marine Protected Areas: Freedom of the High Seas Doctrine and the Common Heritage of Mankind Principle" in Hislop, Cheryle; New, Geoffrey and Bender, Philip *Protecting the Antarctic and Southern Ocean* (University of Tasmania Law School Press, Hobart, 2004) 1.

Holmila, Erkki "Common Heritage of Mankind in the Law of the Sea" (2005) 1 Acta Societatis Martensis 187.

Hudson, Richard "The Scramble for the Seas [From Caracas and Now on to Geneva: The United Nations Third Law of the Sea Conference Whose Original Aim was to Write a Treaty to Govern 'The Common Heritage of Mankind', Finds itself in a Storm of Nationalistic Demands]" (1975) 13(3) War/Peace Report 3.

Jarmache, Elie "La résolution II de l'acte final de la troisiéme conférence des nations unies sur le droit de la mer: le patrimoine commun de l'humanité à l'épreuve du principe de réalité" (1988) 3 Espaces et Ressources Maritimes 19.

Johnston, Douglas "The Common Heritage and the Law of the Sea" in Canadian Council on International Law = Conseil Canadien de Droit International (ed) *International Regulation and Deregulation: Emerging Trends in the Role of International Institutions: Proceedings: XIV Annual Conference: October 17–19, 1985, Ottawa, Ontario = Réglementation et déréglementation internationale: évolution du rôle des institutions internationales: travaux: 17–19 octobre 1985, Ottawa, Ontario* (Canadian Council on International Law, Ottawa, 1986) 237.

Juste Ruiz, José and Castillo Daudí, Mireya "La explotación de la zona de fondos marinos más allá de la jurisdicción nacional (el patrimonio común de la humanidad frente a las legislaciones nacionales)" (1983–1984) 7 Anuario de Derecho Internacional [Universidad de Navarra, Pamplona] 65.

Karti, E "Osnovanie i razmyšlenie: teoriâ prava i resursy dna morej kak obšee nasledie čelovečestva" [Reason and Reflection: Theory of Law and the Resources of the Seabed as the Common Heritage of Mankind] (1991) Sovetskij Ežegodnik Morskogo Prava [Soviet Yearbook of Maritime Law] 32. Russian.

Kent, George "Fisheries and the Law of the Sea: A Common Heritage Approach" (1978) 4(1) Ocean Management 1.

Klimenko, Boris M "Morskoe dno za predelami kontinentel'nogo šel'fa kak obšee dostoânie čelovečestva" [The Seabed Beyond the Limits of the Continental Shelf as Common Heritage of Mankind] in Kolodkin, Anatoly L and Gosudarstvennyĭ Proektno-konstruktorskiĭ i Nauchno-issledovatel'skiĭ Institut Morskogo Transporta 'Soûzmorniiproekt' *Meždunarodno-pravovye problemy mirovogo okeana na sovremennom ètape: sbornik podgotovlen sovmestno s Sovetskoj Associaciej Morskogo Prava i Okeanografičeskim Komitetom Sovetskogo Soûza* [International Legal Problems of the World Ocean at the Present Stage: A Compilation Prepared Jointly with the Soviet Association of Maritime Law and Oceanographic Committee of the Soviet Union] (Transport, Moscow, 1976) 90. Russian.

Knaebe, Timo *The Principle of Common Heritage of Mankind in the New Law of the Sea: An African Perspective Based on Nasila S. Rembe's Work* (GRIN Publishing, Munich, 2007).

Koh, Tommy TB "Deep Seabed Resources Are the Common Heritage of Mankind" in van Dyke, Jon M (ed) *Consensus and Confrontation: The United States and the*

Law of the Sea Convention (Law of the Sea Institute, University of Hawaii, Honolulu, 1985) 228.

Kolodkin, Anatoly L "The Common Heritage of Mankind of the Seabed: The Notion and the Substance" in van Dyke, Jon M (ed) *Consensus and Confrontation: The United States and the Law of the Sea Convention* (Law of the Sea Institute, University of Hawaii, Honolulu, 1985) 241.

Kotz, Steven "The Common Heritage of Mankind: Resource Management of the International Seabed" (1976) 6(1) Ecology Law Quarterly 65.

Krieger, David *The Oceans: A Common Heritage* (Canadian Peace Research Institute, Oakville, 1974).

Logue, John J (ed) *A Rising Wind: The Effort to Revive the Principle of the Common Heritage of Mankind in the Third United Nations Conference on the Law of the Sea* (World Peace Through Law Center, Washington (DC), 1979).
— "The Nepal Proposal for a Common Heritage Fund" (1979) 9(3) California Western International Law Journal 598.
— *The Common Heritage Fund Handbook: Containing Materials Relevant to the Common Heritage Fund Proposal Now Before the Third United Nations Conference on the Law of the Sea* (Common Heritage Institute, Villanova University, Villanova (US), 1981).
— "Moment of Choice: Will the Third World Fight for the Common Heritage Fund Proposal?" in Laursen, Finn (ed) *Toward a New International Marine Order* (Martinus Nijhoff Publishers, The Hague, 1982) 23.
— "Could the Common Heritage Fund Proposal Break the Deadlock in the U.N. Conference on the Law of the Sea?" (1983) 2–3 International Property Investment Journal 283.

Lynch, William C "The Nepal Proposal for a Common Heritage Fund: Panacea or Pipedream?" (1980) 10(1) California Western International Law Journal 25.

McDougal, Myers S and others *The Limits of National Jurisdiction and the Common Heritage Concept: A Panel Discussion* (Woods Hole Oceanographic Institution, Massachusetts, 1973).

Mahmoudi, Said "The Sea, Our Common Heritage" (1999) 91 Naturopa 12.

Malik, A "K voprosu o statuse meždunarodnogo rajona morskogo dna kak obŝego nslediâ čelovečestva" [On the Issue of the Status of the International Seabed Area as the Common Heritage of Mankind] in Zadorožnyj, Georgij P; Koževnikov, Fedor I and Krivčikova, Ėmilija S (eds) *Aktual'nye problemy sovremennogo meždunarodnogo prava. Meždunarodno-pravovye problemy territorii* (Izd-vo MGIMO-Universitet, Moscow, 1980) 81. Russian.

Mann Borgese, Elisabeth "The Seas: A Common Heritage" (1972) 4(2) Center Magazine [Center for the Study of Democratic Institutions, Santa Barbara] 13.
— *The Enterprises: A Proposal to Reconceptualize the Operational Arm of the International Seabed Authority to Manage the Common Heritage of Mankind* (International Ocean Institute, Msida (MT), 1978).
— "The Role of the Seabed Authority in the '80s and '90s. The Common Heritage of Mankind" in Dupuy, René-Jean (ed) *La gestion des ressources pour l'humanité: le droit de la mer = The Management of Humanity's Resources: The Law of the Sea* (Workshop of the Hague Academy of International Law and United Nations University, The Hague, 29–31 October 1981; Martinus Nijhoff Publishers, The Hague, 1982) 35.

Martins Bôto Leite, Alexandre "O patrimônio comum da humanidade e a exploração dos recursos da 'área' no contexto da Convenção de Montego Bay sobre direito internacional do mar" in Menezes, Wagner and others *Estudos de direito internacional: anais do 2° congresso brasileiro de direito internacional* (Jurá Editora, Curitiba (BR), 2005) vol 3, 107.

Mateesco-Matte, Mircéa "Quelques remarques en marge de la Convention de Montego Bay (Jamaïque) sur le nouveau droit de la mer – du 'patrimoine commun de l'humanité' au patrimoine national des etats riverains" (1983) 7 Annuaire de Droit Maritime et Océanique 17.

Matz-Lück, Nele "The Concept of the Common Heritage of Mankind: Its Viability as a Management Tool for Deep-Sea Genetic Resources" in Molenaar, Erik J and Oude Elferink, Alex G (eds) *The International Legal Regime of Areas Beyond National Jurisdiction: Current and Future Developments* (Martinus Nijhoff Publishers, Leiden, 2010) 61.

Mengozzi, Paolo "Common Heritage of Mankind and Exclusive Economic Zone" (1980–1981) 5 Italian Yearbook of International Law 65.
— "Patrimonio comune dell'umanità e zona economica esclusiva" (1982) 202 Archivio Giuridico Filippo Serafini 635.
— "Patrimonio comune dell'umanità e zona economica esclusiva" in Conforti, Benedetto (ed) *La zona economica esclusiva* (A. Giuffrè Editore, Milan, 1983) 117.

Meshal, Reem A "Common Heritage: The Ideals and Realities of the Exploration and Exploitation of the High Seas" (paper presented to the Qatar International Law Conference on International Legal Issues Arising under the United Nations Decade of International Law, Doha, 22–25 March 1994).

Navarro Batista, Nicolás *Fondos marinos y patrimonio común de la humanidad* (Ediciones Universidad de Salamanca, Salamanca (ES), 2000).

Novaković, Stojan M "Zajednička baština čovječanstva u pravu mora" [The Common Heritage of Mankind in the Law of the Sea] in Vukas, Budislav (ed) *Novo pravo mora* [The New Law of the Sea] (Institut za Međunarodno Pravo i Međunarodne Odnose, Sveučilišta u Zagrebu [Institute of

International and Comparative Law, University of Zagreb], Zagreb, 1982) 170. Serbo-Croatian.

— "Common Heritage of Mankind and the UN Convention on the Law of the Sea" in Bulajić, Milan; Pindić, Dimitrije and Marinković, Momirka (eds) *The Charter of Economic Rights and Duties of States: Ten Years of Implementation. The Proceedings of the First Yugoslav International Seminar on Legal Aspects of the New International Economic Order: Beograd, April 11–13, 1985* (Institute of International Politics and Economics/The Macroproject of Institute Consortium on New International Economic Order, Belgrade, 1986) 215.

— "The Common Heritage of Mankind Applied in the System of Exploitation of the Sea-Bed in the UN Convention on the Law of the Sea" in Vukas, Budislav (ed) *Essays on the New Law of the Sea 2* (Institut za Međunarodno Pravo i Međunarodne Odnose, Sveučilišta u Zagrebu [Institute of International and Comparative Law, University of Zagreb], Zagreb, 1990) 227.

Oda, Shigeru "NIEO, Law of the Sea and Common Heritage of Mankind: Some Comments" in Hossain, Kamal (ed) *Legal Aspects of the New International Economic Order* (Frances Pinter Publishers, London, 1980) 171.

Ogley, Roderick C "Caracas and the Common Heritage" [United Nations Conference on the Law of the Sea] (1974) 4(6) International Relations 604.
— *Whose Common Heritage: Creating a Law for the Seabed* (Frances Pinter Publishers, London, 1975).
— "Birth-Pangs or Death-Rattle? The Common Heritage at Geneva" [United Nations Conference on the Law of the Sea] (1975) 5(2) International Relations 876.

Oraison, André "Réflexions générales sur le concept de 'patrimoine commun de l'humanité' en droit international de la mer (le régime juridique de la zone internationale des fonds marins)" (2005) 83(3) Revue de Droit International, de Sciences Diplomatiques et Politiques 249.

Oude Elferink, Alex G "The Regime of the Area: Delineating the Scope of Application of the Common Heritage Principle and Freedom of the High Seas" (2007) 22(1) International Journal of Marine and Coastal Law 143.

Paech, Norman "Von der freiheit der meere zum common heritage of mankind?" (1994) 8(3) Nord-Süd Aktuell: Vierteljahreszeitschrift für Nord-Süd und Süd-Süd Entwicklungen [Deutsches Übersee-Institut, Hamburg] 396.

Pardo, Arvid *The Common Heritage: Selected Papers on Oceans and World Order 1967–1974* (Malta University Press, Valletta, 1975).
— and Mann Borgese, Elisabeth "The Oceans as the Common Heritage of Mankind" in Feather, Frank (ed) *Through the '80s: Thinking Globally, Acting Locally* (World Future Society, Washington (DC), 1980) 135.
— and Mann Borgese, Elisabeth "The Common Heritage of Mankind and the Transfer of Technology" in Mann Borgese, Elisabeth and White, Paul MT (eds) *Seabed Mining: Scientific, Economic, Political Aspects: An Interdisciplinary Manual* (International Ocean Institute, Msida (MT), 1981) 365.

Pastor Ridruejo, José A "La zona internacional de los fondos marinos como patrimonio común de la humanidad: alcance real del principio" in Truyol Serra, Antonio and others *Pensamiento jurídico y sociedad internacional: libro-homenaje al Profesor D. Antonio Truyol Serra* (Centro de Estudios Constitucionales, Universidad Complutense de Madrid, 1986) 921.

Pavićević, Vladimir "The Ocean Floor – The Common Heritage of Mankind" (1970) 20(478) Review of International Affairs (Belgrade) 33.

Payoyo, Peter B "Fishing for the Common Heritage in Straddling and Highly Migratory Fish Stocks" in International Ocean Institute *Training Programme Course Book* (International Ocean Institute, Halifax (CA), 1994).

— *Cries of the Sea: World Inequality, Sustainable Development and the Common Heritage of Humanity* (Martinus Nijhoff Publishers, The Hague, 1997).

Perišić, Zvonko "Common Heritage of Mankind in the United Nations Convention on the Law of the Sea" in Vukas, Budislav (ed) *Essays on the New Law of the Sea* (Institut za Međunarodno Pravo i Međunarodne Odnose, Sveučilišta u Zagrebu [Institute of International and Comparative Law, University of Zagreb], Zagreb, 1985) 289.

Peterson, Susan "The Common Heritage of Mankind? Regulating the Uses of the Oceans" (1980) 22(1) Environment: Science and Policy for Sustainable Development 6.
— "Law of the Sea Negotiations: Are the Oceans Mankind's Common Heritage?" (1980) Current 26.

Piquemal, Alain *Le fond des mers: patrimoine commun de l'humanité* (Centre National pour l'Exploitation des Océans, Paris, 1973).

Pohl, Reinhard (ed) *Seerecht: die schätze des meeres – das gemeinsame erbe der menschheit?* (Magazin-Verlag, Kiel, 1985).

Ponte Iglesias, María T "La zona internacional de los fondos marinos como patrimonio común de la humanidad: una aspiración truncada" in Universidad del País Vasco *Cursos de derecho internacional y relaciones internacionales de Vitoria-Gastéiz 1997 = Vitoria-Gasteizko nazioarteko zuzenbide eta nazioarteko harremanen ikastaroak 1997* (Servicio Editorial de la Universidad del País Vasco, Bilbao (ES), 1998) 177.

Pontecorvo, Giulio "Reflections on the Economics of the Common Heritage of Mankind: The Organization of the Deep-Sea Mining Industry and the Expected Benefits from

Resource Exploitation" (1974) 2(3) Ocean Development and International Law 203.

Reiley, Eldon H "The Common Heritage of Mankind: Ocean Floor Use" (1985) 5(3) California Lawyer 15.

Robles, Alfredo C "The 1994 Agreement on Deep Seabed Mining: Universality vs. the Common Heritage of Mankind" (1996) 12 World Bulletin 20.

Russo, François "Les ressources du fond des mers, patrimoine commun de l'humanité" (1969) 331(11) Études: Revue Fondée en 1856 par des Pères de la Compagnie de Jésus 527.

Saffo, Paul L "The Common Heritage of Mankind: Has the General Assembly Created a Law to Govern Seabed Mining?" (1979) 53(2) Tulane Law Review 492.

Salamanca Aguado, Esther *La zona internacional de los fondos marinos: patrimonio común de la humanidad* (Editorial Dykinson, Madrid, 2003).

Scheiber, Harry N (ed) *Law of the Sea: The Common Heritage and Emerging Challenges* (Kluwer Law International, The Hague, 2000).

Schmidt, Markus G *Common Heritage or Common Burden? The United States Position on the Development of a Regime for Deep Sea-Bed Mining in the Law of the Sea Convention* (Clarendon Press, Oxford (UK), 1989).

Scovazzi, Tullio "Fondi marini e patrimonio comune dell'umanità" (1984) 67(2) Rivista di Diritto Internazionale 249.
— "I fondi marini al di là delle giurisdizioni nazionali quali patrimonio comune dell'umanità" in *Elementi di diritto internazionale del mare* (3rd ed, A. Giuffrè Editore, Milan, 2002) 111.

— "The Concept of Common Heritage of Mankind and the Resources of the Seabed Beyond the Limits of National Jurisdiction" (paper presented to the 10th Session of the International Seabed Authority's Assembly, Expert Panel on Future Directions, Buenos Aires, 26 May 2006).

— "The Principle of Common Heritage of Mankind in International Law of the Sea: Problems and Prospects" in Phang, Siew M and others (eds) *Innovations and Technologies in Oceanography for Sustainable Development* (University of Malaya Maritime Research Centre, Kuala Lumpur, 2006) 327.

— "The Concept of Common Heritage of Mankind and the Genetic Resources of the Seabed Beyond the Limits of National Jurisdiction" (2007) 14(25) Agenda Internacional 11.

Škrk, Mirjam "Skupna dediščina človeštva v pomorskem mednarodnem pravu" [The Common Heritage of Mankind in the Law of the Sea] (1986) 46 Zbornik Znanstvenih Razprav [Compendium of Scientific Studies of the Faculty of Law, University of Ljubljana] 115. Slovenian.

Sremic-Slat, S "The Common Heritage of Mankind Concept in the Law of the Sea" in Constantopoulos, Demetrios S (ed) *The Law of the Sea with Emphasis on the Mediterranean Issues: Thesaurus Acroasium Volume XVII* (Institute of International Public Law and International Relations of Thessaloniki, Thessaloniki (GR), 1991) 745.

Steinacker, Karl *The Legal Principle of the Common Heritage of Mankind and Deep Sea-Bed Mining Outside the U.N. Convention on the Law of the Sea* (Wissenschaftlicher Autoren-Verlag, Berlin, 1985).

Sybesma-Knol, Neri "The 'Common Heritage of Mankind', Ten Years Later: Developments in the Law of the Sea" (1977) 30(6) Studia Diplomatica 669.

Symonides, Janusz "Sea-Bed and Ocean Floor – The Common Heritage of Mankind" (1986) 16 Polish Political Science Yearbook 159.

Tarnacki, Robert "Use of the Area as a Realization of the Principle of the Common Heritage of Mankind in the Light of the 1982 UN Convention on the Law of the Sea" (2007) 24 Revista Europea de Derecho de la Navegación Marítima y Aeronáutica [Universidad de Málaga] 3535.

United Nations Division for Ocean Affairs and the Law of the Sea *The Law of the Sea: Concept of the Common Heritage of Mankind: Legislative History of Articles 133 to 150 and 311(6) of the United Nations Convention on the Law of the Sea* (United Nations, New York, 1996, Sales No.: 96.V.3).

Upadhyay, Shailendra K "Remarks Concerning the Common Heritage Fund Proposal before Negotiating Group #6 during the 1979 New York Session (August 17, 1979)" [United Nations Conference on the Law of the Sea] (1979) 33 Common Heritage 3.

van Dyke, Jon and Yuen, Christopher "'Common Heritage' v. 'Freedom of the High Seas': Which Governs the Seabed?" (1982) 19(3) San Diego Law Review 493.

van Zÿl, Uys "The 'Common Heritage of Mankind' and the 1982 Law of the Sea Convention: Principle, Pain or Panacea?" (1993) 26(1) Comparative and International Law Journal of Southern Africa 49.

Vijay Kumar, Bhasin "India and the Common Heritage Concept in the International Seabed Area" (2004) 86(6) Current Science 783.

Vitzthum, Wolfgang G (ed) *Die plünderung der meere: ein gemeinsames erbe wird zerstückelt* (Fischer Taschenbuch Verlag, Frankfurt, 1981).

Vojtolovskij, G and Šapiro, A "Čto skryvaet pod buržuaznoj interpretacij koncepcii 'mirovoj okean – obŝego naslediâ čelovečestva'" [What Hides Beneath the Bourgeois Interpretation of the Concept of 'World Ocean – Common

Heritage of Mankind'] (1987) 9 Mirovaâ Èkonomika i Meždunarodnye Otnošeniâ [World Economy and International Relations] 88. Russian.

Vosburgh, John A "The Seabed as Common Heritage of Mankind – A Concept of International Law de lege ferenda" in Inter-American Bar Association *Proceedings of the Twentieth Conference: 30 April – 6 May 1977, Atlanta, United States* (Inter-American Bar Association, Washington (DC), 1982) 143.

Wignaraja, Ponna (ed) "Oceans the Common Heritage of Mankind" (1983) 2 Development 1.

Wünsche, Harry "Die neue konvention über das seerecht und das 'gemeinsame erbe der menschheit'" in Graefrath, Bernhard (ed) *Probleme des völkerrechts 1985* (Akademie-Verlag, Berlin, 1985) 303.

Yu, Jia and Ji-Lu, Wu "The Outer Continental Shelf of Coastal States and the Common Heritage of Mankind" (2011) 42(4) Ocean Development and International Law 317.

Zhao, Lihai "The Common Heritage of Mankind: An Important Principle of Contemporary Law of the Sea" (1987) 55 Beijing Da Xue Xue Bao [Journal of Peking University] 76. Chinese.
— *The Common Heritage of Mankind: An Important Principle of Contemporary Law of the Sea* (World Peace Through Law Center, Washington (DC), 1990).

5. CHM in the Antarctic Context

Anton, Donald K "Protecting Antarctica's Marine Environment: Between Sovereign Rights and Common Heritage" (paper presented to the Conference on Whales, Antarctica, Diplomacy and the Law, Australian National University College of Law, Canberra, 4 September 2006).

Ben Al, Tayeh "Est-ce que le pôle sud est un patrimoine commun de l'humanité?" (1996) 1 Revue Algérienne des Sciences Juridiques, Èconomiques et Politiques 180. Arabic.

Francioni, Francesco "Antarctica and the Common Heritage of Mankind" in Francioni, Francesco and Scovazzi, Tullio (eds) *International Law for Antarctica = Droit international de l'Antarctique* (A. Giuffrè Editore, Milan, 1987) 101.

Guyomard, Ann-Isabelle "La protection du patrimoine culturel en Antarctique" in Nafziger, James AR and Scovazzi, Tullio (eds) *The Cultural Heritage of Mankind = Le patrimoine culturel de l'humanité* (Martinus Nijhoff Publishers, Dordrecht, 2008) 687.

Herber, Bernard P "The Common Heritage Principle: Antarctica and the Developing Nations" (1991) 50(4) American Journal of Economics and Sociology 391.

Hussain, Rajmah "The Antarctic: Common Heritage of Mankind?" (paper presented to the Symposium on the Antarctic and the Environment: Future Prospects, Brussels, 9–10 October 1990).
— "The Antarctic: Common Heritage of Mankind?" in Verhoeven, Joe; Sands, Philippe and Bruce, Maxwell (eds) *The Antarctic Environment and International Law* (Graham and Trotman, London, 1992) 89.

Jacobsson, Marie "Asia, Antarctica and the Principle of the Common Heritage of Mankind" in Herr, Richard A and Davis, Bruce W (eds) *Asia in Antarctica* (Centre for Resource and Environmental Studies, Australian National University with Antarctic Cooperative Research Centre, Canberra, 1994) 139.

Joyner, Christopher C "Antarctica and the 'Common Heritage of Mankind'" (paper presented to the 79th Annual Meeting of the American Society of International Law, New York, 25 April 1985).
— "Common Heritage" in *Governing the Frozen Commons: The Antarctic Regime and Environmental Protection* (University of South Carolina Press, Columbia, 1998) 220.

Keyuan, Zou "The Common Heritage of Mankind and the Antarctic Treaty System" (1991) 38(2) Netherlands International Law Review 173.

Kyriak, Michael T "The Future of the Antarctic Treaty System: An Examination and Evaluation of the 'Common Heritage' and 'World Park' Proposals for an Alternative Antarctic Regime" (1992) 7(1) Auckland University Law Review 105.

Loan, Jeffrey "The Common Heritage of Mankind in Antarctica: An Analysis in Light of the Threats Posed by Climate Change" (2004) 1 New Zealand Yearbook of International Law 149.

Malaysia "Antarctica: Common Heritage of Mankind. Malaysian Statement on Antarctica to the Non-Governmental Organisations (NGOs) at the United Nations Delivered on November 17, 1983" (1983) 16(4) Foreign Affairs Malaysia 437.

Menon, Krishna SR "The Scramble for Antarctica: Conflicts over the Riches of a 'Common Heritage'" (1982) World Press Review 11.

Pharand, Donat "L'Arctique et l'Antarctique: patrimoine commun de l'humanité?" (1982) 7 Annals of Air and Space Law = Annales de Droit Aérien et Spatial 415.

Pindić, Dimitrije "Principle of Common Heritage of Mankind as Alternative and Feasible Situation for Future Exploration and Exploitation of Antarctica" in Bulajić, Milan; Pindić, Dimitrije and Marinković, Momirka (eds) *The Charter of Economic Rights and Duties of States: Ten Years of Implementation. The Proceedings of the First Yugoslav International Seminar on Legal Aspects of the New International Economic Order: Beograd, April 11–13, 1985* (Institute of International Politics and Economics/The Macroproject of Institute Consortium on New International Economic Order, Belgrade, 1986) 225.

Pittman, Howard T "Southern Cone Antarctic Claims, Territories and the Ibero-American Club vs. the Common Heritage of Mankind Theory" (paper prepared for the 14th International Congress of the Latin American Studies Association, New Orleans, 17–19 March 1988).

Puri, Rama "Antarctica: Common Heritage of Mankind" in Sharma, RC (ed) *Growing Focus on Antarctica* (Rajesh Publications, New Delhi, 1986) 267.

Smith, Deborah and Pilotte, Eric "Antarctica: CRAMRA, the Common Heritage Principle, and the Madrid Protocol" (1994) World Outlook 101.

Sun, Kuan-Ming "The Antarctic Minerals Regime and the Common Heritage of Mankind" (1989) 10 Sea Changes 67.

Suy, Eric "Antarctica: Common Heritage of Mankind?" in Verhoeven, Joe; Sands, Philippe and Bruce, Maxwell (eds) *The Antarctic Environment and International Law* (Graham and Trotman, London, 1992) 93.

Tenenbaum, Ellen S "A World Park in Antarctica: The Common Heritage of Mankind" (1990) 10(1) Virginia Environmental Law Journal 109.

Thakur, Ramesh and Gold, Hyam "The Antarctic Treaty Regime: Exclusive Preserve or Common Heritage?" (1983) 32(11–12) Foreign Affairs Reports 169.

Triggs, Gillian "Australian Sovereignty in Antarctica: Traditional Principles of Territorial Acquisition versus a 'Common Heritage'" in Harris, Stuart (ed) *Australia's Antarctic Policy Options* (Centre for Resource and Environmental Studies, Australian National University, Canberra, 1984) 29.

Trofimov, Vladimir "Antarctica and the Concept of the Common Heritage of Mankind" in *Legal Status of Antarktica* (Prometey, Moscow, 1990) 49.

United Nations *Protecting the Common Heritage of Antarctica* (United Nations Department of Public Information, New York, 1993).

Zorn, Stephen A "Antarctic Minerals: A Common Heritage Approach" (1984) 10(1) Resources Policy 2.

6. CHM in the Cultural and Natural Heritage Context

Bilderbeek, Simone "The Common Heritage Principle and the World Heritage Principle" in Bilderbeek, Simone (ed) *Biodiversity and International Law: The Effectiveness of International Environmental Law* (IOS Press, Amsterdam, 1992) 86.

Castelli, Maria EE *Protección jurídica del patrimonio cultural de la humanidad* (Bias Editora, Buenos Aires, 1987).

Cordini, Giovanni and Postiglione, Amedeo (eds) *Ambiente e cultura: patrimonio comune dell'umanità. Atti della VII conferenza internazionale ICEF: Paestum, 6–10 giugno 1997* (Edizioni Scientifiche Italiane, Naples, 1999).

Dolzer, Rudolf "Die deklaration des kulturguts zum 'common heritage of mankind'" in Dolzer, Rudolf; Jayme, Erik and Mußgnug, Reinhard (eds) *Rechtsfragen des internationalen kulturgüterschutzes: symposium vom 22./23. juni 1990 im internationalen wissenschaftsforum Heidelberg* (CF Müller Juristischer Verlag, Heidelberg, 1994) 13.

Forrest, Craig "Angkor Wat: The Common Heritage of Humankind? An International Law Perspective" (paper presented to the UNESCO Conference on Angkor Wat: Landscape, City and Temple – A Conference on New Directions in Research at Angkor, Sydney, 17–22 July 2006).
— "Cultural Heritage as the Common Heritage of Humankind: A Critical Re-Evaluation" (2007) 40(1) Comparative and International Law Journal of Southern Africa 125.

Francioni, Francesco; Del Vecchio, Angela and De Caterini, Paolo (eds) *Protezione internazionale del patrimonio culturale: interessi nazionali e difesa del* *patrimonio comune della cultura* (A. Giuffrè Editore, Milan, 2000).

Genius-Devime, Barbara *Bedeutung und grenzen erbes der menschheit völkerrechtlichen kulturgüterschutz* (Nomos, Baden-Baden (DE), 1996).

Kwak, Sun-Young "The Common Heritage of Mankind Principle versus the Cultural Right to Property: The Jikji Controversy" (paper presented to the Annual Meeting of the Western Political Science Association, Oakland (US), 17 March 2005).

LaFranchi, Howard "Saving Places of Unique Importance; A UNESCO Program Works to Preserve the Sites of Mankind's Common Heritage" (1992) 84(168) Christian **Science** Monitor 10.

Lalive, Pierre "Patrimoine culturel national ou patrimoine culturel commun? (questions transfrontieres)" in Hafner, Gerhard and others (eds) *Liber amicorum Professor Ignaz Seidl-Hohenveldern in Honour of his 80th Birthday* (Kluwer Law International, The Hague, 1998) 365.

Merryman, John H "International Art Law: From Cultural Nationalism to a Common Cultural Heritage" (1983) 15(4) New York University Journal of International Law and Politics 757.

Monden, Anneliese and Wils, Geert "Art Objects as Common Heritage of Mankind" (1986) 19(2) Revue Belge de Droit International = Belgian Review of International Law 327.

Müller, Markus "Kulturgüterschutz: mittel nationaler repräsentation oder wahrung des gemeinsamen erbes der menschheit?" in Fechner, Frank; Oppermann, Thomas and Prott, Lyndel V (eds) *Prinzipien des kulturgüterschutzes: ansätze im deutschen, europäischen und internationalen recht* (Duncker and Humblot, Berlin, 1996) 257.

Nafziger, James AR and Scovazzi, Tullio (eds) *The Cultural Heritage of Mankind = Le patrimoine culturel de l'humanité* (Martinus Nijhoff Publishers, Dordrecht, 2008).

Phelan, Marilyn E "The Concept of a Cultural Heritage of Humanity" in Phelan, Marilyn E (ed) *The Law of Cultural Property and Natural Heritage: Protection, Transfer and Access* (Kalos Kapp Press, Evanston (US), 1998) 1.

Prott, Lyndel V "A Common Heritage: The World Heritage Convention" in Macinnes, Lesley and Wickham-Jones, Caroline R (eds) *All Natural Things: Archaeology and the Green Debate* (Oxbow Books, Oxford (UK), 1992) 65.

Scovazzi, Tullio "La notion de patrimoine culturel de l'humanité dans les instruments internationaux" in Nafziger, James AR and Scovazzi, Tullio (eds) *The Cultural Heritage of Mankind = Le patrimoine culturel de l'humanité* (Martinus Nijhoff Publishers, Dordrecht, 2008) 3.

Seidl-Hohenveldern, Ignaz "Artefacts as National Cultural Heritage and as Common Heritage to Mankind" in Bello, Emmanuel G and Ajibola, Bola A (eds) *Essays in Honour of Judge Taslim Olawale Elias* (Martinus Nijhoff Publishers, Dordrecht, 1992) 163.

Šošić, Trpimir M "The Common Heritage of Mankind and the Protection of the Underwater Cultural Heritage" in Vukas, Budislav and Šošić, Trpimir M (eds) *International Law: New Actors, New Concepts – Continuing Dilemmas. Liber amicorum Božidar Bakotić* (Martinus Nijhoff Publishers, Leiden, 2010) 319.

Strati, Anastasia "Deep Seabed Cultural Property and the Common Heritage of Mankind" (1991) 40(4) International and Comparative Law Quarterly 859.
— "The Implication of Common Heritage Concepts on the Quest for Cultural Objects and the Dialogue Between North and South" in American Society of International Law

Proceedings of the 89th Annual Meeting: New York, April 5–8, 1995 (ASIL, Washington (DC), 1995) 439.

Turner, Stefan "Cultural Property as National Heritage and Common Human Heritage: The Problem of Reconciling Common and Individual Interests" in Prott, Lyndel V (ed) *Witnesses to History: Documents and Writings on the Return of Cultural Objects* (UNESCO, Paris, 2009) 110.

Zaragoza Huerta, José and Aguilar Cavallo, Gonzalo "El desafío de la diversidad cultural como patrimonio de la humanidad = The Challenge of Cultural Diversity as Heritage of Mankind" (2007) 5 Letras Jurídicas: Revista Electrónica de Derecho 1 <http://letrasjuridicas.cuci.udg.mx>.

7. CHM in the Climate Context

Busuttil, Salvino "The Statement by the Director-General of the Foundation for International Studies on Climate as the Common Heritage of Mankind" in Attard, David J *Climate Change* (Foundation for International Studies, University of Malta, Valletta, 1989) 21.

Calderón Hinojosa, Felipe [President of Mexico] "La preservación de nuestro patrimonio común: en busca de un acuerdo justo para combatir el cambio climático" (paper presented to the 16th U Thant Distinguished Lecture, United Nations University, Tokyo, 2 February 2010).

Mercure, Pierre-François "Le choix du concept de développement durable plutôt que celui du patrimoine commun de l'humanité afin d'assurer la protection de l'atmosphère" (1996) 41(3) McGill Law Journal 595.

Ramakrishna, Kilaparti "North-South Issues, Common Heritage of Mankind and Global Climate Change" (1990) 19(3) Millennium: Journal of International Studies 429.
— "North-South Issues, Common Heritage of Mankind and Global Climate Change" in Rowlands, Ian and Greene, Malory (eds) *Global Environmental Change and International Relations* (Macmillan in association with Millennium, Basingstoke (UK), 1992) 145.

Tabone, Censu "Conservation of Climate as Part of the Common Heritage of Mankind: A Verbatim Record of the Speech by Dr Censu Tabone as Malta's Minister of Foreign Affairs at the Thirty-Fifth Meeting Held at Headquarters, New York, on Monday, 24th October 1988 at 10.00 a.m." in Borg, Simone (ed) *Malta's Initiative on Climate Change* (Ministry of Foreign Affairs, and Ministry for Resources and Rural Affairs in collaboration with the University of Malta, Valletta, 2009) 3.

van Hoorick, Geert "The Principle of Common Heritage and Climate Change Policy" (paper presented to the Climate Change Conference, Lviv (UA), 3–4 December 2009).

Westing, Arthur H "The Atmosphere as a Common Heritage of Humankind" (1989) 2(3) Peace and the Sciences 78.
— "The Atmosphere as a Common Heritage of Humankind: Its Role in Environmental Security" (1994) 34(4) Scientific World 5.

8. CHM in the Biodiversity Context

Agarwal, Anil and Narain, Sunitha "Common Heritage of the Genetic Pool: The Challenges Thrown Up by the Convention on Biodiversity" in Rajagopalan, R (ed) *Common Heritage and the 21st Century: Proceedings of Pacem in Maribus XXV: November 1997* (International Ocean Institute in cooperation with the Foundation for International Studies and Government of Malta, Mside (MT), 1998) 127.

Altieri, Miguel A and Nicholls, Clara "Sementes nativas: patrimônio da humanidade essencial para a integridade cultural e ecológica da agricultura camponesa" in Carvalho, Horácio M (org) *Sementes: patrimônio do povo a serviço da humanidade* (Editora Expressão Popular, São Paulo, 2003) 159.

Aoki, Keith "Reclaiming 'Common Heritage' Treatment in the International PGR Regime Complex" (paper presented to the IPMG Workshop on Intellectual Property: Biotechnology Capacity and Development, Buenos Aires, 25–27 September 2006).
— "Overlapping International Legal Regimes for Plant Genetic Resources: From 'Common Heritage' to 'Sovereign Property'" in *Seed Wars: Controversies and Cases on Plant Genetic Resources and Intellectual Property* (Carolina Academic Press, Durham, 2008) 61.
— and Luvai, Kennedy "Reclaiming 'Common Heritage' Treatment in the International Plant Genetic Resources Regime Complex" (2007) 1 Michigan State Law Review 35.

Brush, Stephen B "The Demise of 'Common Heritage' and Protection for Traditional Agricultural Knowledge" (paper presented to the Conference on Biodiversity, Biotechnology and the Legal Protection of Traditional Knowledge, St. Louis (US), 4–6 April 2003).

— "The Demise of 'Common Heritage' and Protection for Traditional Agricultural Knowledge" in McManis, Charles R (ed) *Biodiversity and the Law: Intellectual Property, Biotechnology and Traditional Knowledge* (Earthscan, London, 2007) 297.

Footer, Mary E "Our Agricultural Heritage: Sustainability, Common Heritage and Intergenerational Equity" in Schrijver, Nico and Weiss, Friedl (eds) *International Law and Sustainable Development: Principles and Practice* (Martinus Nijhoff Publishers, Leiden, 2004) 433.

Genetic Resources Communications Systems (Laboratory for Information Science in Agriculture) "Genetic Resources: From Common Heritage to Sovereign Resource: Changing Concepts of Genetic Resources: Special Issue on CBD COP 4 and the 10th Global Biodiversity Forum" (1998) 14(1–2) Diversity 11.

Giovannetti, Manuela "Biodiversità delle sementi: bene privato o patrimonio dell'umanità?" (2009) 65(6) Il Ponte: Rivista di Politica Economia e Cultura Fondata da Piero Calamandrei 97.

Hermitte, Marie-Angèle "La gestión de un patrimonio común: la diversidad biológica" in Barrere, Martine (ed) *La tierra: patrimonio común* (Paidós, Barcelona, 1992) 181.

Joly, Pierre-Benoît "Du patrimoine commun à la privatisation des ressources génétiques" (1992/05) 458 Le Monde Diplomatique 10.

Kawano, Kazuo "Crop Genetic Resource as Common Human Heritage and its Utilization" (2004) 41 Gamma Field Symposia [Institute of Radiation Breeding, Ministry of Agriculture and Forestry, Japan] 1.

Kloppenburg, Jack R and Kleinman, Daniel L "Seed Wars: Common Heritage, Private Property and Political Strategy" (1987) 95 Socialist Review 7.

— "Plant Genetic Resources: Common Heritage or National Sovereignty?" (1988) 4(1–2) GeneWatch 10.

— "Seeds of Controversy: National Property versus Common Heritage" in Kloppenburg, Jack R (ed) *Seeds and Sovereignty: The Use and Control of Plant Genetic Resources* (Duke University Press, Chapel Hill (US), 1988) 173.

— "Seed Wars: Common Heritage, Private Property, and Political Strategy" in Socialist Review Collective (ed) *Unfinished Business: 20 Years of Socialist Review* (Verso, New York, 1991) 139.

Mercure, Pierre-François "Le rejet du concept de patrimoine commun de l'humanité afin d'assurer la gestion de la diversité biologique" (1995) 33 Canadian Yearbook of International Law = Annuaire Canadien de Droit International 281.

Mgbeoji, Ikechi "Beyond Rhetoric: State Sovereignty, Common Concern, and the Inapplicability of the Common Heritage Concept to Plant Genetic Resources" (2003) 16(4) Leiden Journal of International Law 821.

Prathapan, Kaniyarikkal D and Priyadarsanan, Dharma R "Biological Diversity: A Common Heritage" (2011) 46(14) Economic and Political Weekly 15.

Ranganathan, Radha "Plant Genetic Resources for Food and Agriculture: A Common Heritage of Mankind?" (paper presented to the International Chamber of Commerce, Panel Discussion on Making Intellectual Property Work for Development, Geneva, 26 April 2007).

Segura Roda, Isabel "Los recursos fitogenéticos como patrimonio común de la humanidad: implicaciones jurídicas de dicha consideración" (1985) 1(1) Revista de Derecho Agrario y Alimentario [Asociación Española de Derecho Agrario, Madrid] 55.

Thomas, Frédéric "Biodiversité, biotechnologies et savoirs traditionnels. Du patrimoine commun de l'humanité aux ABS (Access to Genetic Resources and Benefit-Sharing)" (2006) 188 Revue Tiers Monde 825.

Trotti, John L "Compensation versus Colonization: A Common Heritage Approach to the Use of Indigenous Medicine in Developing Western Pharmaceuticals" (2001) 56(3) Food and Drug Law Journal 367.

Wood, David "Crop Germplasm: Common Heritage or Farmers' Heritage?" in Kloppenburg, Jack R (ed) *Seeds and Sovereignty: The Use and Control of Plant Genetic Resources* (Duke University Press, Chapel Hill (US), 1988) 274.

9. CHM in the Human Genome Context

Bedjaoui, Mohammed "Le génome humain comme patrimoine commun de l'humanité: ou la génétique de la peur à l'espérance" in M'Baye, Kebe and Vasak, Karel (eds) *Federico Mayor amicorum liber: solidarité, égalité, liberté = solidaridad, igualdad, libertad = solidarity, equality, liberty: le livre d'hommage offert au Directeur Général de l'UNESCO par ses amis a l'occasion de son 60e anniversaire* (Bruylant, Brussels, 1995) vol 2, 905.

Bovenberg, Jasper A "DNA as Universal Property. Mining the Common Heritage of Our DNA: Lessons Learned from Grotius and Pardo" in *Property Rights in Blood, Genes and Data: Naturally Yours?* (Martinus Nijhoff Publishers, Leiden, 2005) 35.
— "Mining the Common Heritage of Our DNA: Lessons Learned from Grotius and Pardo" [2006] Duke Law and Technology Review 008 <http://dltr.law.duke.edu>.

Byk, Christian "A Map to a New Treasure Island: The Human Genome and the Concept of Common Heritage" in Fujiki, Norio and Macer, Darryl RJ (eds) *Bioethics in Asia: The Proceedings of the UNESCO Asian Bioethics Conference (ABC'97) and the WHO-assisted Satellite Symposium on Medical Genetics Services, 3–8 Nov, 1997 in Kobe/Fukui, Japan; 3rd MURS Japan International Symposium, 2nd Congress of the Asian Association of Bioethics, 6th International Bioethics Seminar in Fukui* (Eubios Ethics Institute, Christchurch (NZ), 1998) 26.
— "A Map to a New Treasure Island: The Human Genome and the Concept of Common Heritage" (1998) 23(3) Journal of Medicine and Philosophy: A Forum for Bioethics and Philosophy of Medicine 234.

de Faramiñán Gilbert, Juan M "Los bienes intangibles de la especie humana (el genoma humano como patrimonio común de la humanidad)" (2000) 2(5) Rivista della

Cooperazione Giuridica Internazionale [Istituto Internazionale di Studi Giuridici, Milan] 12. Reprinted from Trindade, Antônio AC and Swinarski, Christophe (eds) *Héctor Gros Espiell amicorum liber: persona humana y derecho internacional = Personne humaine et droit international = Human Person and International Law* (Bruylant, Brussels, 1997) vol 1, 311.
— "El genoma humano como patrimonio de la humanidad" in Romeo Casabona, Carlos M (ed) *Biotecnología, desarrollo y justicia* (Editorial Comares, Granada, 2008) 187.

Falcone, Anna "Genetica e nuovi diritti fondamentali: dalle dichiarazioni internazionali a salvaguardia del genoma umano all'innovazione delle costituzioni nazionali: verso una tutela globale del patrimonio genetico dell'umanità" (2009) 60 Persona y Derecho [Universidad de Navarra, Pamplona] 271.

Ghoshray, Saby "Interpreting Myriad: Acquiring Patent Law's Meaning Through Contemporary Jurisprudence and Humanistic Viewpoint of Common Heritage of DNA" (2011) 10(3) John Marshall Review of Intellectual Property Law 508.

Gros Espiell, Héctor "El patrimonio común de la humanidad y el genoma humano" (1995) 3 Revista de Derecho y Genoma Humano = Law and the Human Genome Review 91.
— "The Common Heritage of Mankind and the Human Genome" in Suy, Eric and Wellens, Karel (eds) *International Law: Theory and Practice: Essays in Honour of Eric Suy* (Martinus Nijhoff Publishers, The Hague, 1998) 519.

Ida, Ryuichi "Human Genome as Common Heritage of Humankind – With a Proposal" in Fujiki, Norio and Macer, Darryl RJ (eds) *Bioethics in Asia: The Proceedings of the UNESCO Asian Bioethics Conference (ABC'97) and the WHO-assisted Satellite Symposium on Medical Genetics*

Services, 3–8 Nov, 1997 in Kobe/Fukui, Japan; 3rd MURS Japan International Symposium, 2nd Congress of the Asian Association of Bioethics, 6th International Bioethics Seminar in Fukui (Eubios Ethics Institute, Christchurch (NZ), 1998) 59.

Knoppers, Bartha M "Le génome humain: le patrimoine commun de l'humanité?" (paper presented to the Les Grandes Conférences, Musée de la Civilisation de Québec, Québec, 7 December 1998).
— *Génome humain: le patrimoine commun de l'humanité?* (Éditions Fides, Montréal, 1999).
— "The Human Genome: Individual Property or Common Heritage?" in Mattei, Jean-François (ed) *Ethical Eye: The Human Genome* (Council of Europe Publishing, Strasbourg, 2001) 109.

Kutukdjian, Georges B "Le génome humain: patrimoine commun de l'humanité" in Huber, Gérard (ed) *Cerveau et psychisme humains: quelle éthique? = Human Brain and Psyche: Which Ethics?* (Èditions John Libbey Eurotext, Paris, 1996) 245.
— "Le génome humain: patrimoine commun de l'humanité" in Trindade, Antônio AC and Swinarski, Christophe (eds) *Héctor Gros Espiell amicorum liber: persona humana y derecho internacional = Personne humaine et droit international = Human Person and International Law* (Bruylant, Brussels, 1997) vol 1, 601.

Liuzzi, Antonella "Genetic Information. Individual or Common Heritage?" (2002) 29(2) Sociologia del Diritto 9.

López Moreno, Angeles and López Hueso, Félix "El proyecto genoma humano: ¿patrimonio de la humanidad?" (1999–2000) 94 Revista de la Facultad de Derecho de la Universidad Complutense 219.

Ossorio, Pilar N "Common Heritage Arguments and the Patenting of DNA" in Chapman, Audrey R (ed) *Perspectives on Gene Patenting: Religion, Science, and*

Industry in Dialogue (American Association for the Advancement of Science, Washington (DC), 1998) 89.
— "The Human Genome as Common Heritage: Common Sense or Legal Nonsense?" (2007) 35(3) Journal of Law, Medicine and Ethics 425.

Resnik, David B "The Human Genome: Common Resource But Not Common Heritage" in Korthals, Michiel and Bogers, Robert J (eds) *Ethics for Life Scientists* (Springer, Dordrecht, 2005) 197.

Spectar, Jem M "The Fruit of the Human Genome Tree: Cautionary Tales about Technology, Investment, and the Heritage of Humankind" (2001) 23(1) Loyola of Los Angeles International and Comparative Law Review 1.

Sturges, Melissa L "Who Should Hold Property Rights to the Humane Genome? An Application of the Common Heritage of Humankind" (1997) 13(1) American University International Law Review 219.

10. CHM in the Shared Water Resources Context

Aït-Kadi, Mohamed; Shady, Aly M and Szöllösi-Nagy, Andras (eds) *Water, The World's Common Heritage. Proceedings of the First World Water Symposium: Marrakesh, Morocco, 21–22 March 1997* (Elsevier Science Publishers, Kidlington (UK), 1997).

Belaïdi, Nadia "The 'Common Heritage': A Legal Concept to Combine Past-Present-Future. Example of Water Management" (paper presented to the 5th Conference of the International Water History Association, Tampere (FI), 13–17 June 2007).
— and Euzen, Agathe "De la *chose commune* au patrimoine commun. Regards croisés sur les valeurs sociales de l'accès à l'eau" (2009) 37(145) Mondes en Développement 55.

Centre Tricontinental (Louvain-la-Neuve) *L'eau, patrimoine commun de l'humanité* (L'Harmattan, Paris, 2001).

Diouf, Jacques "L'eau, patrimoine de l'humanité" in Aït-Kadi, Mohamed; Shady, Aly M and Szöllösi-Nagy, Andras (eds) *Water, The World's Common Heritage. Proceedings of the First World Water Symposium: Marrakesh, Morocco, 21–22 March 1997* (Elsevier Science, Kidlington (UK), 1997) 103.

Martin-Nagle, Renee "Fossil Aquifers: A Common Heritage of Mankind" (2011) 2 George Washington Journal of Energy and Environmental Law 39.

Petit, Olivier and Romagny, Bruno "La reconnaissance de l'eau comme patrimoine commun: quels enjeux pour l'analyse économique?" (2009) 145(1) Mondes en Développement 9.

Petrella, Riccardo "L'eau, patrimoine commun de l'humanité parce que droit fondamental" (paper presented to the Les Grandes Rencontres du Cégep Limoilou, Québec, 11 April 2000).
— "L'eau, patrimoine commun de l'humanité parce que droit fondamental" (2002) 20(78) Chimie Nouvelle 58.
— and others "L'eau, bien commun de l'humanité" (2000) 50 Le Monde Diplomatique 16.

Polet, François "El agua, apuesta global de futuro: ¿privatización o patrimonio común de la humanidad?" in Amin, Samir and Houtart, François (eds) *Globalización de las resistencias: el estado de las luchas 2003* (Icaria Editorial, Barcelona, 2003) 201.

Thill, Georges and Jean-Pierre, Ezin (eds) *L'eau, patrimoine mondial commun: co-expertise scientifique, participative et gouvernance* (Presses Universitaires de Namur, Namur (BE), 2002).

Fondation de Malte

The Fondation de Malte was originally formed in 1998 through the inspiration of Mrs Mercedes Busuttil and registered in Malta by Public Deed. The Fondation de Malte is an international NGO, based in Malta, dedicated to cultural affairs, environmental concerns, education and human rights. It acts through the organisation of seminars, conferences, courses and publications.

Its objectives as outlined by its statute are:

- To stimulate and manage international research, training and information programmes relating primarily to global and regional issues, sustainable development, human rights, tolerance and peacekeeping;
- To administer national, regional and international projects having a bearing on the Fondation's aims;
- To offer consultancy and related services in pursuit of the above objectives;
- To provide multi-cultural and multi-lingual educational programmes, especially at a tertiary level with high academic standards and to co-operate with similar institutes in the promotion and running of such programmes and courses, including study and research bursaries;
- To undertake such other activities, especially the dissemination of information and publications, as are likely to contribute to the Fondation's vocation;
- To embark on any project or programme which furthers these objectives including co-operation with entities, national or international, embracing similar or related pursuits.

Fondation de Malte
Casa Cintraj, 54 West Street, Valletta, VLT 1536, Malta
Email address: info@fondationdemalte.org
Website: www.fondationdemalte.org

EurOcean

EurOcean is a focal point for information on marine science and technology in Europe and its Internet portal (www.eurocean.org<http://www.eurocean.org/>) is aiming to provide information on topics related to marine science and technology in Europe with a priority given to three main domains: Marine Knowledge (Identification and transference), Marine Research Infrastructures (Identification and maximization) and Communication and Education Activities on Marine Sciences. EurOcean contributes to the initiatives aiming to implement a Marine European Research Area and a European maritime policy.

The creation of an European Organisation for Information on Marine Science and Technology results of a joint French - Portuguese initiative to implement the recommendations of the report "Towards a new marine dimension for Europe through research and technological development
<http://www.eurocean.org/np4/file/58/Towards_Marine.pdf>",
adopted on 4th May 2000 by a group of governmental experts from 15 European countries. EurOcean has presently 14 Full Members from 9 European Countries and 3 Cooperating Members including Fondation de Malte.

EurOcean
European Centre for Information on Marine Science and Technology
Avenida Dom Carlos I, 126-2°, 1249-074, Lisbon, Portugal
Email address: eurocean@fct.mctes.pt
Website: www.eurocean.org